Cutting Through the

The Right Employee Engagement Strategies for YOU

Norma Dávila and Wanda Piña-Ramírez

Photo credits: Photo by Eric Stella for The Barcore. Styling by Luis Santiago Collazo for The Creative Mind—Media and Style Group. Photo used with permission.

ASTD Press is an internationally renowned source of insightful and practical information on workplace learning, performance, and professional development.

ASTD Press
1640 King Street Box 1443
Alexandria, VA 22313-1443 USA

Ordering information: Books published by ASTD Press can be purchased by visiting ASTD's website at store.astd.org or by calling 800.628.2783 or 703.683.8100.

Library of Congress Control Number: 2013951095

ISBN-10: 1-56286-863-2
ISNB-13: 978-1-56286-863-5
e-ISBN: 978-1-60728-602-8

ASTD Press Editorial Staff:
Director: Glenn Saltzman
Manager and Editor, ASTD Press: Ashley McDonald
Community of Practice Manager, Workforce Development: Ron Lippock
Editorial Assistant: Ashley Slade
Text and Cover Design: Lon Levy and Ana Foreman

Printed by The PA Hutchison Company, Mayfield, PA, www.pahutch.com

To:
Manuel and Mamma

To:
Frank, Nelsi, Mami, Tere,
Abuelo Lelo, Papi Rafi,
Padre Domingo

From Us:
Luis Santiago

Contents

Foreword vii

Preface xi

Acknowledgments xv

Part I: Getting Started With Employee Engagement 1
    Chapter 1: Myths and Realities of Employee Engagement 5
    Chapter 2: Importance of Organizational Culture and Context
        in Employee Engagement 25

Part II: The Process of Employee Engagement and Its Steps:
        Engagement "I" Path 49
    Chapter 3: Starting Out and Testing the Waters 55
    Chapter 4: Stable and Critical Incident 73
    Chapter 5: Growth and Decline 93
    Chapter 6: Stay or Leave and Re-engage or Disengage 111

Part III: Employee Engagement Throughout the Employee's Career:
        Career "I" Path 133
    Chapter 7: Just Beginning, Getting Settled, and Looking for More 139
    Chapter 8: Riding the Tide, Mission Accomplished, and Moving On 159

Part IV: Bringing It All Together 181
    Chapter 9: From Generic to Individual Attention:
        Are You Practicing What You Preach? 185
    Chapter 10: Next Steps and Action Planning
        in Employee Engagement 207

References 219

About the Authors 221

Index 223

FOREWORD

When you devote yourself to excellence in everything you do, you begin to feel a greater sense of positive pride about the way you are conducting your days. This in turn increases self-respect and confidence, which, in turn, release greater energy and passion. You begin to feel good about yourself. People who feel good about themselves do great work and create remarkable things. And this, in turn, just makes them raise their standards of excellence even higher. It's an upward spiral that takes people to ever-increasing places of joy, meaning, and internal peace.

—Robin Sharma

What is employee engagement? What is its relevancy for managers and businesses? How has the definition of the word *engagement* changed with the new generation of employees? Will you, as a manager, be able to achieve your goal of engaging your employees? Even if you do, to what extent will they be engaged? What does engagement mean to these employees?

The book that you are about to read is not really a book in a classic sense of that word. It is much more than a mere book. It is an invaluable instrument for you to use in the process of assessing and developing the real, actual level of engagement of your workforce.

Cutting Through the Noise: The Right Employment Engagement Strategies for YOU was conceived, designed, developed, and written with one major purpose and objective: to provide managers with a full and comprehensive understanding of the true meaning of the term *employee engagement*, and its importance for your business.

The book is not necessarily designed to be read from cover-to-cover. It is a practical, easy-to-understand working manual, in which you will find multiple ideas and reflections that will lead you to challenge and maybe even deconstruct your preconceptions about the meaning of the term *engagement*, as we know it. As you read, you will feel, correctly, that your assumptions are carefully but aggressively questioned and that you may need to break away from the paradigms by which you have operated your business and managed your people in the past.

This process of deconstructing paradigms starts immediately, in chapter 1, where the authors dare you to answer a "fact or myth" questionnaire concerning multiple statements. The answer will open your eyes, as well as your company's, into a self-discovery voyage that will undoubtedly lead you to a new manner in which you conduct your business.

The book takes you on a journey, starting with the authors defining organizational culture as "the attitudes, beliefs, values, expectations, knowledge, language, opportunities, structure, and materials of a particular workplace that define how business is conducted on a daily basis." Furthermore, for each one of these characteristics, you will find hypothetical situations for you to evaluate and consider possible courses of action.

In the end, the journey will take you to the ultimate goal of turning the managers into role models for employee engagement. To achieve this goal, you and your company need to understand and accept change. Change is a process. Since awareness certainly precedes change, you will learn that in order to be able to change something, you need to really pay attention to it, and overcome the fear that accompanies any change.

During that voyage, multiple tables, checklists, and Listen up! notes will maintain you in the correct path toward your goal. The authors truly deliver an understanding that the pillars of employee engagement are trust and respect, that listening is "hearing what they are not saying," and the fact that, "one size does not fit all." The book achieves its purpose and, if you as a reader and manager are really "engaged" in the learning process, you will elevate the level of success of your company, as well as yourself.

A study made by ISR Global Research in 2006 demonstrates that employee engagement directly affects your company's bottom line. Simply put, companies with high levels of employee engagement will, most likely, be financially superior to those with low levels of employee engagement.

In sum, it is crystal clear that ignoring the importance of achieving high levels of employee engagement is not a choice in today's economy. This book will guide you through the correct path in your journey in search for the highest level of employee engagement in your company.

Yldefonso López-Morales, Esq.

Preface

Now more than ever we hear that employee engagement is a thing of the past. We are not sure if this is true, but we are certain that people do not become engaged in the same way as they did before. We believe that people do become engaged, but what has changed is to whom do we become engaged and how do we handle that engagement.

The question is: How do employees become engaged?

In years past, engagement was more directed at "names" and "brands." However, as employees and management have developed closer relationships, those relationships have gained value and importance. As a manager or business owner, you are fundamental for the growth, maintenance, maturity, and sustainability of engagement in your company as well as with your employees.

Consider these possible scenarios:

» You are a manager, were a manager, or will be a manager.

» You want to know and understand more about employee engagement.

» You are aware of the importance of employee engagement for your business and for your employees.

» You are ready to challenge your own assumptions and take a good look at yourself and your own level of engagement.

» You are looking for a workbook that will sometimes validate your thinking and other times challenge it, and which is based on the experiences of other practitioners like you.

» You were asked to "do something about those engagement results before the next employee survey."

» You are looking for ideas about how you can contribute to increase employee engagement either through management practices or through learning and development.

» You believe that you can make a difference in your employees' lives.

» You want to support your business to increase employee engagement.

» You are ready for an interactive experience.

If any of these scenarios seem familiar or if you are (or intend to be) a manager, a leader, or both, and you are looking for practice-driven suggestions to increase employee engagement, this book is for you.

We acknowledge the importance of different types of books about employee engagement that are currently available for you. Therefore, before we explain further what this book is, it is important for us to clarify what this book is not.

This book is not a review of statistics and research on employee engagement. It is not a presentation of case studies about employee engagement. It is not a lengthy exposition about theories of employee engagement.

Consider this book a guide and a workbook for you to apply what you learn to your particular circumstances in your organization, company, or workplace. Although we cite examples of the work of others who have studied employee engagement, this book is primarily based on our experiences working with managers from different organizations in various roles. Thus, it is directed to meet your needs of information and reflection as you go through each one of the chapters.

As firm advocates of the importance of "using what we learn as soon as we learn it so that we do not forget it," each chapter contains questions and exercises for you to interact with the content as if we were sitting somewhere with you, perhaps having a cup of coffee or tea, talking about employee engagement. Every chapter contains sections named "Now it's your turn" for you to answer questions or to complete a table, checklist, or develop a plan to help you think. Every chapter also includes "Listen Up!" notes, which are tidbits of information that you should remember as you continue your journey. At the end of each chapter, you will find a summary of the main points that we have discussed.

We are also advocates of the power of stories as learning tools. Therefore, we have included examples to illustrate various points throughout the book.

These examples are entirely hypothetical and do not portray any particular organization or individual. They are composites of different individuals and organizations that we built based on our experiences.

Although we would like you to read this book in its entirety, we understand that you may be particularly interested in some topics that stand out for you. If that is the case, we invite you to return to the beginning of the book later.

This is your book. Use it in the way that makes more sense to you.

Let's begin our journey.

Norma Dávila and Wanda Piña-Ramírez

Acknowledgments

This project started out as an idea and became what you have been reading as a result of the good wishes and deeds of many individuals who provided guidance, support, and feedback over several months. A word, a gesture, a reference, a text message, or a joke was sometimes all we needed to shift our thinking or stretch our limits. When we did not see the light at the end of the tunnel, they were already throwing a party on the other side of the tunnel. When we needed to take a break from our work, they were there for us. When we could not find typographical errors or see if something made sense, they read, read, and read the manuscript and helped us to improve it—thinking about what you, the manager or business owner, our intended reader, would find useful.

Our special thanks to:

» Manuel and Frank, our husbands, thank you for understanding the sounds of silence when we were in the beginning, middle, and end of our creative process. Your engagement throughout our ride and our path paid off.

» Yldefonso (Ylde), the first endorser of this project who saw the gleam in our eyes when it was just a dream and unequivocally told us that writing it was the right thing to do. We are glad that we listened to you.

» Ramón Rivera-Grau, for believing in us and in the value of what we do.

» Alfredo Carrasquillo, for guiding Wanda to find her answers when the book was not yet a book.

» Tere and Nelsi, for your patience to wait for the best time to read, read, and read the manuscript in all of its forms so that your comments would be most useful. We cannot imagine having a better team of readers and support group.

Acknowledgments

- » Luis Santiago, for envisioning our future.

- » Simón and Magaly, for supporting Wanda each one in your unique way.

- » Manuel Bermúdez, for your support and trust in Wanda's ideas along the way.

- » Kurt Schindler and Clara Pérez O'Neill, for knowing when to ask and how to ask about our progress. Your words kept Norma focused on the future.

- » Ron Lippock, Manager of ASTD's Workforce Development Community, for guiding us through the process of turning our idea into a book; and to the team at ASTD Press for ensuring that the final product met the standards that you deserve.

- » Ashley McDonald, Manager of ASTD Press, for being more than an editor and being open to learn with us about engagement.

- » Our past and present clients who inspired us to create.

- » All those managers and their direct reports who are, in one way or another, represented throughout the book's stories and examples.

- » All those people who, in one way or another, knowingly or unknowingly, helped us to turn thoughts into an outline that became countless drafts of what you are reading today.

It's an ending and a beginning.

Norma and Wanda

PART I

Getting Started With Employee Engagement

Introduction

The first two chapters of this book set the stage for the work that you will do—with our guidance—to take a different look at employee engagement and what you can do to strengthen it among your employees. They are the beginning of our journey with you.

In chapter 1, we invite you to look at your understanding and ideas of what engagement is and what it is not; later, we share with you our definition of what engagement is and encourage you to come up with your own. We further ask you to assess your own engagement. We also discuss the factors that contribute to move engagement in a particular direction (drivers). We close the chapter with some statistics to place engagement in its broader context, emphasizing its importance and impact for you, your employees, and your business.

In chapter 2, we introduce our definition of organizational culture, the relationship between the individual and the culture, and individual differences within a culture. We also begin to explore your role as a manager to promote employee engagement within your organization's culture.

Let's begin.

CHAPTER 1:

Myths and Realities of Employee Engagement

Before we start this journey, let's see what you think about employee engagement. Review the statements in Worksheet 1.1 and place a check mark or an "x" under the corresponding column if you think the statement is fact or myth. We will review your answers shortly.

Worksheet 1.1   Facts and Myths of Employee Engagement

STATEMENT	FACT	MYTH
When employees are more engaged, they are more loyal to the company.		
When employees are less engaged, they have more absenteeism.		
Older employees tend to be more engaged than younger employees.		
More skilled employees tend to be less engaged than less skilled employees.		
Men tend to be more engaged than women.		
Employees who work from home are less engaged than those who do not.		
Employees who work in shifts are more engaged than those who work regular hours.		
Recognition fosters engagement.		
Performance evaluations do not contribute to engagement.		
Communication promotes engagement.		

STATEMENT	FACT	MYTH
The work environment promotes engagement.		
Interactions with peers promote engagement.		
Managers are critical to foster engagement.		
If an employee has more control over the environment, he is more engaged.		
Healthy people are less engaged.		
Promotions always foster employee engagement.		
Engagement is all about the money.		
Engagement is not at all about the money.		
Engagement is all internal.		
Engagement is all external.		
Only one definition of engagement exists.		
The world around employees does not have an impact on their level of engagement.		
Employee engagement stays the same throughout an employee's career.		
Major events or critical incidents do not affect employee engagement.		
Employees are always engaged with the workplace and their manager.		

Now let's see how your answers compare with the answers that we expected, as shown in Worksheet 1.2.

Worksheet 1.2   Facts and Myths of Employee Engagement— Expected Answers

STATEMENT	FACT	MYTH
When employees are more engaged, they are more loyal to the company.	X	
When employees are less engaged, they have more absenteeism.	X	
Older employees tend to be more engaged than younger employees.	X	
More skilled employees tend to be less engaged than less skilled employees.	X	
Men tend to be more engaged than women.		X
Employees who work from home are less engaged than those who do not.		X

STATEMENT	FACT	MYTH
Employees who work in shifts are more engaged than those who work regular hours.		X
Recognition fosters engagement.	X	
Performance evaluations do not contribute to engagement.		X
Communication promotes engagement.	X	
The work environment promotes engagement.	X	
Interactions with peers promote engagement.	X	
Managers are critical to foster engagement.	X	
If an employee has more control over the environment, he is more engaged.	X	
Healthy people are less engaged.		X
Promotions always foster employee engagement.		X
Engagement is all about the money.		X
Engagement is not at all about the money.		X
Engagement is all internal.		X
Engagement is all external.		X
Only one definition of engagement exists.		X
The world around employees does not have an impact on their level of engagement.		X
Employee engagement stays the same throughout an employee's career.		X
Major events or critical incidents do not affect employee engagement.		X
Employees are always engaged with the workplace and their manager.		X

1. How many did you answer correctly?

_____

_____

_____

2. How many did you answer incorrectly? Which ones?

_____

_____

_____

3. What stands out from your correct and from your incorrect answers?

    _____

    _____

    _____

    _____

4. What other facts or myths about employee engagement are common in your company?

    _____

    _____

    _____

    _____

We encourage you to review the results of this exercise, as well as your answers to other questions that we will present throughout the book, to continue your journey toward playing a more active role in the development of engagement among your employees.

LISTEN UP!

Employees decide if they want to be engaged.

What Engagement Is for Us and for Them: It's All About the "I"

We have reviewed some facts and myths about engagement. Before we delve into this topic, we'll discuss how we define engagement, based on our experience working with clients as well as on our research about this topic. We will continue to ask questions to continue to guide your thinking about engagement.

In our definition: *Engagement is the business's backbone and the result of the psychological contract plus the experience that exists between employee and employer. The foundation of employee engagement is respect, trust, and performance. Engagement is dynamic as it changes over the course of an employee's tenure at a workplace and overall career as a consequence of multiple events and factors that we will discuss. Engagement is intrinsic and individual. In conclusion, engagement is all about "I."*

Engagement is a voluntary connection to the business and to its purpose; it includes an emotional component to the workplace in order to achieve its desired outcomes. Employees decide if they want to be engaged. Thus, even though employee engagement entails an emotional connection, it also involves a rational component as the employee decides whether or not to be engaged given her individual circumstances. We have concluded that, even though many workplaces may seem to be similar, they are as unique as the individuals who belong to them, which in turn affects what it means for employees to be engaged with the organization.

As you may expect, the definitions and explanations of employee engagement are as varied as the authors who have proposed them; however, they have some similarities. These definitions include emotional, rational, and practical features that are connected to engagement's impact on businesses as well as on employees. In general, these definitions refer to engagement as voluntary. Each well-known definition includes these important components; in addition, there are other factors that contribute to move employee engagement in a particular direction. These factors are typically known as drivers of engagement.

LISTEN UP!

Each organization needs to define and understand employee engagement in its own terms.

Drivers of Engagement

We have found different types of drivers of engagement. As a manager, you will use some of these drivers to influence your employees' engagement. We will refer again to these drivers in other chapters where we describe the Engagement "I" Path and the Career "I" Path. Please keep in mind that the impact of these drivers does not happen in isolation; the company's context and culture will mitigate or compound their impact on employee engagement.

Manager-Employee Relationship

The manager-employee relationship is the most important driver of employee engagement; this relationship has been tied to employees' satisfaction or dissatisfaction with their work or workplace and their subsequent decision of whether to stay in the workplace or go elsewhere. How you communicate with your employees and what you communicate to them are central issues in the relationship that lies at the heart of the psychological contract we mentioned in our definition of engagement. Therefore, you as a manager have the interesting challenge of forming genuine yet professional relationships with your employees that will benefit the company, the employee, and you.

We have already established that employee engagement has a solid emotional component because engagement is all about "I" (me) and my circumstances. Therefore, employees need to acquire a strong sense of purpose and autonomy in their work even when they may not control the final decision, product, or outcome. This sense of purpose and autonomy is directly tied to their ownership of their work.

LISTEN UP!
Employees do not leave their companies. They leave their managers.

Intrinsic Motivation

Intrinsic motivation, defined by Thomas (2009), as "a sense of meaningfulness and of progress" (98), will lead the employee to find value in what he does and to establish that emotional connection without depending on external factors, such as many mentioned in this section. In our work we have found several examples of employees who remain engaged with their workplaces or managers mainly as a result of their strong intrinsic motivation that often takes them through otherwise challenging times.

Leadership

Leadership has different meanings in different companies. Leadership is an important driver of engagement that goes beyond job titles, because not all managers are leaders and not all leaders are managers. A manager like yourself (and others in the company at all levels), has an important responsibility in fostering employee engagement. This responsibility comes through in how you enable your employees to do their work, how you conduct yourself, and how you, as a role model, convey messages through different channels. Our interpretation of a leader is someone who drives people to a common purpose and brings confidence to her team, with the point to make things happen beyond herself. You do not need a title to be a leader.

LISTEN UP!

"People buy into the leader before they buy into the vision."
—John C. Maxwell

Performance Management

Performance management is an area related to management that affects employee engagement. For us, performance management includes goals and objectives, as well as how work is distributed to meet company goals. It is an ongoing process that starts when an employee is hired and ends when he leaves the company. As an ongoing process, performance management serves as the company's platform to align the employee's actions and behaviors to meet those company goals. Performance management comprises resource allocation, workplace flexibility, and work-life balance, as well as measures of an employee's progress in achieving the desired results. In addition, how high- and low-performing employees are managed, as well employees' perceptions of equity and justice, are included in this driver.

LISTEN UP!

"Let your performance do the thinking."—H. Jackson Brown, Jr.

Career Development

Career development is another driver of engagement. Even though most employees, especially those who belong to the younger generations, will have several positions at several companies throughout their work lives, those changes are career development. Its meaning may have changed for different groups, but long-term career potential and promotion opportunities are still as relevant today as they were many years ago. These issues are important because they relate to an employee's intent to stay in the workplace and the resulting decision will have an impact on the business.

An employee who finds opportunities for growth and development within a company will acquire a stronger sense of loyalty to that company and to you as a manager for facilitating those opportunities. This employee will be more likely to intend to stay in the company for a longer period of time and to dedicate that additional time and effort that is often needed to obtain results. Therefore, you as a manager must pay particular attention to the career development needs of your employees and help them to set realistic expectations for their future. At the same time, you should ensure that you match the right employee with the right opportunity at the right time. Don't be afraid of losing your best employees to other departments or divisions, because if they do not find what they need working with you, they will be more likely to leave your workplace altogether to go somewhere else. Minimize your losses. Keep the big picture of engagement in mind.

Financial and External Incentives

Even though employee engagement extends beyond financial and external incentives, these are still important drivers and need to be considered. Base pay, incentive pay, and total rewards are particularly significant in the current (and recent) economic climate where companies have had to implement tighter controls on costs, including pay and benefits, to survive. Total rewards, defined by World at Work (2011) as "the programs, practices, elements, and dimensions that collectively define an organization's strategy to attract, motivate, and retain employees" (4), will also play a key role. Employees still focus considerable attention to their compensation and benefits packages when they make a decision to stay in a company or to go elsewhere.

> **LISTEN UP!**
>
> "Incentives make people do things they never imagined they could do."—Wanda Piña-Ramírez

Organizational Image

Shifting our discussion to external components of engagement, we look at organizational image. The view that employees and the outside world have in their minds about an organization and how they feel about an organization becomes the organizational image. In today's work environment, employees are particularly aware of a company's image and reputation. The emotional connection that employees feel with their company is composed of how others see it from the outside and how employees see it from the inside. As individuals seek a place to work, they are very much aware of its reputation and how others perceive it because, by joining the company, they are overtly endorsing what it stands for. Let's look at these examples.

Pablo is very environmentally conscious. He would be attracted to a company known for implementing green programs. Pablo would be very pleased in a paperless environment.

Danielle is very structured and formal; she would be drawn to hierarchical workplaces where roles and responsibilities are clearly defined. Danielle would feel more comfortable in an environment with a strict business dress code.

Steven is focused on creating new ideas that could become profitable products. He would be interested in a company that values results more than processes and procedures and where no one pays particular attention to his choice of attire. Steven would be happy wearing jeans or even shorts, weather permitting, every day.

Each of these individuals, with their varying personalities, would likely choose a different organization to join.

Brand Alignment

Brand alignment is another driver related to organizational image. With today's availability of information through multiple channels, often accessed simultaneously, it is very easy for an employee to find out if the company is acting consistently with its brand, or what makes it unique among its competitors. For example, a company that prides itself on its community orientation and service would be initially appealing to an employee who likes to spend time working for the common good. Any contradiction between what the company says it would do and what it actually does would have a negative impact on that employee's engagement. In this example, if the company's real connection with the community is limited to only collecting funds for nonprofit groups, the service-oriented employee will feel disappointed and will, very likely, begin to feel disengaged after joining the company. Brand alignment ensures that people know and understand an organization's brand and purpose and that they demonstrate that they "live the brand" in everything that they do, everywhere that they do it, and every time that they do it.

LISTEN UP!

"Brand alignment is living the brand."—Wanda Piña-Ramírez

In this section, we discussed different drivers that contribute to overall employee engagement. Although many believe that an employee's relationship with a company is essentially an exchange of services for goods, our experience has shown other dimensions of the workplace, such as manager-employee relationship and the "I" factor, contribute to employee engagement. We would now like you to reflect on what we just discussed.

Now it's your turn.

Let's look at your definitions of employee engagement.

1. What is your definition of employee engagement?

2. How is your definition of employee engagement similar or different from your company's definition?

3. Think about our definition of engagement and write your new definition of engagement.

Your answers to these questions will help you understand where you are as you promote engagement among your employees. This is your first step in this journey.

Let's test your "I."

1. Am I engaged?

       _____

       _____

       _____

2. How engaged am I?

       _____

       _____

       _____

3. What does "being engaged" mean to me?

       _____

       _____

       _____

4. Do I care about engagement?

       _____

       _____

       _____

5. Am I engaged to my manager or to my workplace? Am I engaged to both or to none? Why?

       _____

       _____

       _____

       _____

       _____

6. What are my expectations about engagement?

_____

_____

_____

7. What do I need to be engaged? (Describe in as much detail as possible.)

_____

_____

_____

8. What drives my engagement?

_____

_____

_____

Now let's test your Company "I."

1. What drives engagement in your company?

_____

_____

_____

2. What drives engagement for your employees?

_____

_____

_____

3. Does your company care about employee engagement?

_____

_____

_____

_____

4. What initiatives in employee engagement is your company taking?

_____

_____

_____

5. Is your company measuring employee engagement?

_____

_____

_____

6. What steps is your company taking with those employee engagement measures?

_____

_____

_____

7. As a manager, are you accountable for employee engagement?

_____

_____

_____

8. Who is responsible to drive employee engagement in your company?

_____

_____

_____

In the next section, we share with you a review of general trends in employee engagement that may be useful to you as you place employee engagement in your company in a broader context.

Trends in Employee Engagement: Some Statistics

Books about engagement typically include large amounts of statistics and data, but we said at the beginning that this book would not do so. However, we would like to place trends in employee engagement in a broader context. Please keep in mind that measures and methods may appraise engagement differently because they are based on individual operational definitions of engagement. Here are some statistics for you to keep in mind.

According to Aon Hewitt (2011), globally, 60 percent of employees were engaged in 2009, but 56 percent of employees were engaged in 2010. The authors consider this change as the largest decline in engagement in 15 years and attribute it to shifts in specific industries, such as financial, and in specific regions, such as Asia-Pacific, Europe, and North America regions.

According to Towers Watson (2012), globally, 35 percent of employees are highly engaged (that is they have high scores on traditional engagement, energy, and enablement); 22 percent of employees are unsupported (are traditionally engaged, but lack either enablement or energy); 17 percent of employees are detached (have either enablement or energy, but do not have traditional engagement); and 26 percent of employees are disengaged (have low scores on the three attributes). Similarly, Harter (2012) reports that 30 percent of United States workers are engaged in their work and workplace, 52 percent are not engaged, and 18 percent are actively disengaged. Based on the reports of these authors, the majority of workers are not engaged in their jobs.

We have found differences in employee engagement depending on education, age, and gender among employees with comparable income levels. Specifically, those employees who have high school or higher degrees are less likely to be engaged than those with less than a high school degree or some college education. Employees who have higher education tend to have more options for mobility and, consequently, they tend to have less engagement. Therefore, companies need to dedicate more efforts to retain these employees. Employees who are between the ages of 30 to 50 are less likely to be engaged than older employees; those employees who are between the ages of 50 to 60 are seeking stability in their lives and those who are over age 60 are embracing stability. In the economic climate of the 2010s, we are seeing more employees who are over the age of 70 staying active in the workforce, reinventing themselves, and evolving dramatically. Further, because of changes in family structures that have led many women to become the primary wage earners of their families, women tend to be more engaged than men and tend to stay with the same organization longer.

Job-related factors, such as job role and length of time at position, are indicators of employee engagement. In our experience, professional employees tend to be more engaged than nonprofessional employees regardless of educational attainment. By professional employees we mean those who look at their employment as a career instead of as a job and who have made considerable investments, often in terms of time, money, and effort, to build their present and future. Typically, professional employees are salaried employees who tend to look for career paths and other growth opportunities within companies and who are not satisfied with remaining in one position throughout their entire working lives. From our point of view, more than half of employees are disengaged by the time they reach three years at their jobs; at this time they often begin to look for what to do next, either in their current company or elsewhere. This question of "What should I do next?" arises every three to five years of service.

Before we shift our attention to our next topic, we would like you to reflect on what we have shared with you in this section.

Now it's your turn.

Let's look at measures and trends in employee engagement to help you to calibrate employee engagement in your company.

1. How do you measure employee engagement in your team?

2. What is your team's level of employee engagement?

3. How does your company's level of employee engagement compare with that of your competitors?

    _____

    _____

    _____

    _____

4. Has your company's level of employee engagement changed over the last three to five years, or has it remained consistent?

    _____

    _____

    _____

5. To what do you attribute any changes in engagement over the last three to five years?

    _____

    _____

    _____

6. Are there any differences in employee engagement between groups such as professionals and nonprofessional workers?

    _____

    _____

7. Are there any differences in employee engagement between supervisors, senior managers, and individual contributors?

    _____

    _____

    _____

8. Are there any differences in employee engagement between groups such as those who have a high school education or higher and those who have less than a high school education?

    _____

    _____

    _____

9. Are there any differences in employee engagement between genders?

    _____

    _____

    _____

10. To what do you attribute any differences in employee engagement between groups?

    _____

    _____

    _____

Impact of Employee Engagement

The ways to measure and analyze the impact of employee engagement on businesses, as well as on employees, are as varied and diverse as the studies conducted to identify this impact. Metrics depend on each industry, but all industries have financial indicators. Customer satisfaction and employee turnover are usually good indicators of business impact. Engagement may be an important predictor of a company's health, and often organizations that report higher levels of employee engagement continue to outperform those that report lower levels of engagement. In this section, we highlight the impact of employee engagement on businesses and then on employees.

On Businesses

According to Hewitt Associates (2010), those companies with higher levels of engagement have a base from which to build engagement further, and those that do not continue to lose ground in engagement. Aon Hewitt (2012) presented that the best employers average 20 percent higher engagement than other employers; and companies in the top quartile of the best employers in 2012 had 50 percent higher total shareholder return than the average company. So overall, addressing the issue of employee engagement makes business sense.

On Employees

Engagement seems to serve as a filter when employees are handling difficult work situations such as crises, layoffs, and mergers. For example, we have seen highly engaged employees come together during times of an organizational crisis because of their sense of ownership and belonging; less engaged employees may resist working additional hours or may resent taking pay cuts for the benefit of the greater good. We have also found that highly engaged employees may perceive layoffs, particularly those as a result of a merger, differently than less engaged employees. Highly engaged employees may feel a greater sense of loss than less engaged employees because they were more emotionally invested in the company and they believe that the company owes something to them as part of that psychological contract that we have mentioned previously in this chapter.

Engagement also seems to contribute to overall employee well-being since more engaged employees tend to experience higher levels of well-being than those who are not engaged. In our experience, how employees handle work-related stress tends to be related to their levels of engagement, as more engaged employees tend to handle stress better than less engaged employees.

Now it's your turn.

Let's look at the impact of employee engagement on your company.

1.   What has been the impact of employee engagement on your company?

_____

_____

_____

_____

2.   What has been the impact of employee engagement on the employees of your company?

_____

_____

_____

_____

3.   Are there any differences in the impact of employee engagement on your company based on any particular situations?

_____

_____

_____

_____

KEY POINTS AND TAKEAWAYS

- Engagement is the backbone of the business.
- Take into consideration the employee's psychological contract with the company.
- Engagement is all about the "I" (me) and my circumstances.
- Consider the manager-employee relationship.
- Engagement has a solid emotional component.
- Keep in mind factors such as education, gender, and roles, among others.
- Engaged companies outperform those that report lower levels of engagement.

CHAPTER 2:

Importance of Organizational Culture and Context in Employee Engagement

In this chapter, we take a closer look at the importance of the organizational culture and context in which employees function on a day-to-day basis and its role in their engagement. We also begin to explore your role as a manager to promote engagement among your employees within that culture.

What Is Organizational Culture?

We define an organization's culture as the attitudes, beliefs, values, expectations, knowledge, language, opportunities, structure, and materials of a particular workplace that define how business is conducted on a daily basis. An organization's culture is the cumulative result of the combination of these elements over time; it is dynamic, changing as the organization grows and transforms itself. An organization's culture further sets the overall climate of the organization and becomes a major factor in employees' desire to join, stay, and grow in the organization. We will look at each one of these elements individually as well as at its impact on employee engagement.

Attitudes

Attitudes play a critical role on engagement because they include emotional (how I feel), behavioral (what I do), and cognitive (how I think) components.

These components are shared easily among employees through personal or online contact. Together, the expression of these elements, by employees as well as managers, can have a powerful influence on the engagement of other employees who learn from each other and eventually may adopt similar attitudes. Let us analyze a hypothetical situation.

It's Friday! You and your team have worked throughout the week on a project. You have been looking forward to the weekend (how I feel) because you want to spend some time with your family. You arrive at work earlier than usual (what I do) because this is the best way to get a head start on your day (how I think). You find out that there is an unanticipated need to work over the weekend and your plans will have to change. As you mentally reorganize your day and your weekend, you meet several of your peers in the hallway. They talk about how miserable they are because they have to ask their employees to work over the weekend (how I feel). They also tell you that they are going to ask their employees to work over the weekend by email to avoid personal contact (what I do). They further share that they think that it was unfair of the company to make such a last minute request (how I think).

The possible outcomes of this situation shed light on the cascade effect that individuals' attitudes can have on others. You could adopt the attitudes of your peers and behave as they are; or you could continue to work with your employees as you always have, even though you have to change your plans. As a manager, your employees will learn about how you feel, what you do, and how you think, and very likely, they will align themselves to you. Your attitudes will influence their attitudes, and eventually, their level of engagement; if something is important for you, it should be important for them and vice versa.

LISTEN UP!

"Monitor your attitude."
— Wanda Piña-Ramírez

Beliefs

Beliefs are internal representations of what individuals think is true. Beliefs are "I" representations of events. An example of a commonly held belief in the workplace is that working after regularly scheduled hours is a sign of loyalty. Acting on the basis of this belief, managers praise employees who tend to work after regularly scheduled hours and criticize those employees who do not. Informally, groups may show admiration for those employees whose actions are consistent with this belief and disparage those whose actions do not, with comments such as "he is always looking at the clock" or "she never stays a minute after 5:30 p.m." Team interpersonal relations may become strained as a result of how employees act upon this belief. It may eventually affect their level of engagement as employees will gravitate toward groups that share their beliefs about this issue among many others.

LISTEN UP!

Beliefs are the results of experiences, assumptions, ideas, theories, and conclusions.

Values

Values represent the essence of what is important for the company, and as such, are often showcased prominently in corporate offices for everyone to read. Values embody what is not negotiable for the company. Values are typically included in employee onboarding documents to ensure that new employees become familiar with them upon their start in their new positions and that the new employees' actions are consistent with them. Statements of values may include passion, excellence, innovation, motivation, and team-work among others.

Having a values statement is a step in the right direction, but it is not enough to ensure congruence between company values and managers' actions; managers at all levels should demonstrate these values as they conduct business every day. Let's see an example.

A company that includes innovation in its values statement may encourage all employees to propose ideas to improve customer service. Managers may analyze employee proposals to select which ones could be implemented and attribute the success to the employee who proposed the idea. In contrast, managers could reject proposals with responses such as "we already tried that before and it did not work," or "we do not do business that way," thus discouraging further proposals from employees. Consequently, the value of innovation will have completely different meanings depending on how managers respond to employee efforts at creating something new. The level of support for those efforts will have an impact on employee engagement as employees tend to repeat behaviors that will produce positive outcomes for them and tend to develop an emotional attachment with entities that support them.

Employees bring their own personal beliefs and values into the workplace. Managers also select employees who have something in common with them. Be aware of this tendency. The experience of sharing these beliefs and values among all employees and managers can create strong bonds between them and can thus influence engagement because, as we have shown in the examples in this chapter, these beliefs and values will guide employees' actions. This perceived similarity will strengthen that emotional connection with the company that will drive the employee to do more than is expected of him.

LISTEN UP!

"Values are contagious."
— Norma Dávila

Expectations

Employees begin to form expectations about the workplace during the recruitment and onboarding processes as they learn about what the organization stands for and how it treats its employees; their experiences later either validate or destroy those initial ideas. Employee expectations are part of the psychological contract established between employee and employer that also includes the manager-employee relationship. Let's see an example.

Todd was told during the recruitment process that he would be granted more responsibilities in projects after his 90-day probationary period. Todd's performance during his first project contributed to its completion before the deadline and several thousand dollars under budget; his contributions were the subject of an article in the company's newsletter. When Todd asked Sheila, his manager, about his responsibilities in his next assignment, he was surprised to learn that he would not have any new responsibilities.

After overcoming the usual disappointment associated with not receiving more responsibilities, Todd looked for ways to improve his performance and to make even more contributions in the second project to ensure that he would receive what was offered to him for the third project. Assuming that his performance in the second project is exemplary again, if Todd receives those additional responsibilities for his third project, he will conclude that his expectations were met and he will be more likely to continue driving himself to higher levels of performance. If, on the contrary, Todd's third project includes the same level of responsibility as the previous two, he will conclude that his expectations were not met and he will either maintain a stable level of performance or his performance will begin to decline because his expectations were not met. Todd's level of engagement will also change depending on whether or not his expectations are met.

LISTEN UP!

"Expectations are always there."
— Norma Dávila

Knowledge

Knowledge includes the technical components of the work itself as well as the unwritten rules of how to conduct business. Many employees have enough understanding of the technical side of their work as a result of their education, training, or experience; employers may provide whatever knowledge employees still need through training and other means. However, employees acquire knowledge about the unwritten rules from their managers, their peers, or their networks. Those unwritten rules are indispensable for success in any work environment and may have a greater effect on an employee's career than subject matter expertise if they are not learned correctly and promptly. "This is how we do things at RulesForever" and "Let me show you the Rules-Forever way" are common phrases used during new employee onboarding. Any behavior outside of the boundaries delineated by those rules is usually not accepted and may even bring negative consequences for the wrongdoer, including exclusion from sources of information and power. Employees who feel confident about their mastery of these types of knowledge are more likely to have higher levels of engagement than those who do not.

Language

Language, in its verbal and nonverbal forms, is another important element of an organization's culture that serves to bring together its employees because of their shared understanding of its meaning. Employees may initially feel lost when they join a company that uses multiple acronyms or shorthand to communicate; this is particularly the case when the same acronym has different industry-specific meanings. Here are some examples of acronyms that can have multiple meanings: POB can mean post office box or place of birth; NSF can denote not sufficient funds or national science foundation; OD can signify overdraft or organizational development; PM stands for project management and performance management; HR represents hour, high rate, or human resources.

LISTEN UP!

Excessive use of acronyms can be annoying, particularly for newcomers.

Language use contributes to define group membership within a company because choice of words and vocabulary typically reflect background and experience. Let's see an example of what happens in companies related to use of language and its impact.

Patricia is a certified Project Management Professional (PMP) and uses phrases such as *phase review* and *free float* in casual conversation. Jeremy, Patricia's manager, does not have that certification and, even though he participated in her selection as a team member and the certification was a requirement for the position, he often interprets her word choices as a way to stand out. Jeremy is concerned about the impression that Patricia's word choice is making on how others perceive her, because this will affect her integration into the team in a negative way. Jeremy needs to maintain team cohesion, but he cannot afford to lose a valuable resource like Patricia. As a manager, Jeremy can preserve the engagement by speaking with Patricia so that she becomes aware of the need to make herself be understood by others. Jeremy also needs to support and demonstrate that he values diversity in the team, and by doing so, he would be promoting engagement in the team.

Similarly, misinterpreting the meaning of nonverbal language used by others, such as glances and distance, may interfere with someone's team integration and engagement. Let's see an example.

Kim works in a cubicle environment. Upon her arrival at her work area, Kim noticed that her peers wore earplugs to work and that Nicole, her manager, needed to touch them gently on their shoulders to introduce Kim. When she asked, Nicole told Kim that the team agreed to work with earplugs as a way to maintain silence so that they could concentrate on their tasks and complete them on time. For this team, wearing earplugs was a way of saying "do not disturb," but they were willing to make exceptions, such as when meeting a new member. By quickly learning and understanding the meaning of nonverbal cues in her team, Kim feels connected to them and, very likely, her level of engagement will increase faster than if she were feeling isolated.

LISTEN UP!

Your role as a manager is to provide the meaning of verbal and nonverbal communication.

Opportunities

Opportunities include options to grow and develop within a company. These may entail projects, assignments, trainings, acknowledgments, and promotions, among others. They may exist inside the company or outside of it, for example, at a professional association or other relevant group. How these opportunities become available and to whom are issues considered by employees in terms of their relationship with the company. Let's see an example.

Your-Risk-Is-Ours Insurance prides itself in the importance of employee development and has a higher than average per capita training cost in its industry. To an outsider, Your-Risk-Is-Ours Insurance is the perfect place to work, learn, and grow. However, when the employees of Your-Risk-Is-Ours Insurance completed an engagement survey, they stated that they perceived that external candidates were preferred over internal candidates for new positions, that only members of certain groups received promotions, and that the same employees always received rewards and recognitions. Not surprisingly, their level of engagement was very low for a company of its size because its employees perceived inequities and did not see any reason to go beyond the minimum that was expected from them.

Therefore, managers need to pay special attention at availability of opportunities as an element of culture and its impact on employee engagement, as opportunities are often included in operational definitions of engagement.

LISTEN UP!

Be aware of perceptions.

Structure

Structure denotes how work is organized in the workplace. Structure influences how employees interact with each other and with their managers and supervisors, defining the real level of formality expected and accepted in those interactions. Let's look at two examples.

PaperClipsForAll has seven management levels (team leader, supervisor, manager, assistant vice president, associate vice president, vice president, and president). All employees must address management by title and last name and all communication must be channeled through immediate supervisors. PaperClipsForAll does not have an "open door policy" because such a policy is considered a waste of valuable time and resources. At PaperClipsForAll, all employees know exactly what they need to do because their roles and responsibilities are clearly defined, as is the progressive discipline process when employees do not comply.

In contrast, RollOurOnlyWay Brands has three management levels (team leader, manager, and director) and everyone addresses everyone else by first name. At RollOurOnlyWay Brands, all employees are encouraged to communicate with anyone in the company at any time and by any means. RollOurOnlyWay Brands defines roles and responsibilities in general terms to promote flexibility and innovation in completing tasks and projects.

In these two examples, structure determines employee autonomy and defines interaction norms; in turn, these two factors lead to dissimilar levels of employee engagement for each company.

Processes and procedures are linked with structure because they establish how work is completed in organizations and guide its completion through official channels. Since employees are expected to follow processes and procedures on a daily basis, management needs to address any deviations from what is established. Very likely, employees at PaperClipsForAll are required to adhere to every detail of every procedure; while, in contrast, those at RollOurOnlyWay Brands are encouraged to challenge every procedure to find ways to complete tasks more efficiently. As we mentioned before, how work is completed is a driver of employee engagement; employees at PaperClipsForAll and RollOurOnlyWay Brands could be expected to have divergent levels of engagement.

LISTEN UP!

An element of the culture can destroy or build your employees' engagement.

Materials

Materials refer to what resources employees have available to do their jobs. These may include, but are not limited to: equipment, computers, software, devices, uniforms, protection, furniture, and supplies. Companies decide which materials they will provide to employees and which ones they will be required to provide for themselves and under what circumstances. In some instances, employees receive stipends and other allowances to subsidize costs of materials. Let's look at two examples of the importance of materials within organizational culture and its impact on employee engagement.

Eva is a master of technology. Imagine her in the following scenarios.

WeAreExpeditious LLC offers consulting services in technology solutions. WeAreExpeditious LLC migrates to the latest versions of software when they become available, practicing what they preach. WeAreExpeditious LLC upgrades its computers every three to five years. At the main office of WeAreExpeditious LLC, consultants have high-quality furniture and resources to work; they use office supplies on an honor system.

WeTatter4U does not change versions of programs or software until they become obsolete. Some computers at WeTatter4U have less memory than many cellphones and, consequently, cannot run many current software versions. WeTatter4U is proud of how it reuses and recycles office furniture and partitions after remodeling areas or relocating staff.

Where do you think that Eva would be more engaged?

In these two examples, access to materials and resources conveys to employees how much management values them, and, accordingly influences levels of employee engagement.

Now it's your turn.

Worksheet 2.1 presents our depiction of the relationship between the different elements of organizational culture that we just discussed on employee engagement. On a scale of 1 to 10, where 1 has the lowest value and 10 has the highest value, assign a value to each element of culture indicating how relevant you perceive them to be as factors that influence employee engagement in your team.

Worksheet 2.1 **Elements of Organizational Culture and Employee Engagement**

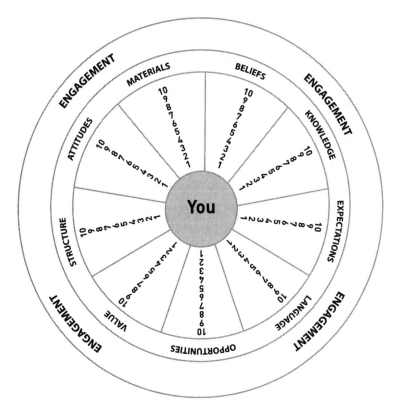

Evaluate each score and determine why you chose that score.

1.   Which elements received the highest scores?

_____

_____

_____

_____

2.   Which elements received the lowest scores?

_____

_____

_____

_____

3.   What do you need to do to reach the desired outcomes?

_____

_____

_____

_____

Now you have a clearer picture of how your company's culture affects your engagement. We invite you to complete the same exercise with your employees so that you can learn about how your company's culture affects their engagement.

Please think about your company's culture as you answer the following questions.

1.   How would you describe your company's culture as it is related to employee engagement?

_____

_____

_____

_____

2.   Do you agree or disagree with your company's culture? Why?

_____

_____

_____

3.   How would you describe the relationship between your
     company's culture and you as a manager?

_____

_____

_____

4.   How do you see yourself as a manager within that culture?

_____

_____

_____

5.   Do you know your company's values?

_____

_____

_____

6.   How familiar are you with your company's acronyms?

_____

_____

_____

7.   Does your company's structure help or hinder your work
     as a manager? Why?

_____

_____

_____

We invite you to share this exercise and its results with your employees as a way to obtain more information about what is important for them and for you about organizational culture and its impact on employee engagement.

Importance of Organizational Culture

Employees spend approximately one-third of their days at their workplaces or completing work-related activities, even if they work remotely. As a result of these working hours, employees spend more time with co-workers and managers than with their families, thus having multiple experiences in common with colleagues under relatively controlled circumstances. When employees are at work, they have common workspaces, share work breaks, use similar tools, and speak a common language, among other collective experiences. Although the Internet and social media allow employees to be exposed to a wide range of external information, many workplaces restrict access to those media during working hours. Thus, because of the exposure to external sources of information or to individuals with different backgrounds, these shared experiences have additional weight on employee perceptions of their workplaces as well as on their behavior. These shared experiences and the context where they take place play a role in modifying employee engagement. This socialization process continues and changes throughout an employee's tenure at that employer.

Organizational culture provides direction and establishes common grounds as well as defines interactions. Through its culture, a company promotes employee teamwork and loyalty. A company also encourages retention through its reputation that is a by-product of its culture.

Now it's your turn.

1. Do you believe that the impact of organizational culture on employee engagement stays the same or that it changes over time? Why?

_____

_____

_____

2. What three steps are you taking to ensure that the culture of your company supports employee engagement?

_____

_____

_____

The Relationship Between Individuals and Organizational Culture

We discussed the importance of organizational culture and shared examples of how each one of its components contributes to employee engagement. We described organizational culture as dynamic at the beginning of our discussion; we now propose that the relationship between individuals and organizational culture is also dynamic as both influence each other over time. Let's look at an example to illustrate what we mean.

Joyce, a manager known for introducing changes gradually, recently joined HugePills Pharmaceuticals to lead its accounting department. HugePills Pharmaceuticals has a reputation of being a traditional organization. Joyce went through the typical onboarding process and soon started to hear phrases like "we have always done it this way," and "this is how we do things in HugePills." She also received "well-intended warnings" about how long she would last in her position if she continued asking questions to change how the department operates.

Joyce was determined to make a difference at HugePills Pharmaceuticals. She became thoroughly knowledgeable about how her department operated, ensuring the collaboration of well-respected informal leaders. She spent considerable time with her staff formally as well as informally getting to know them and developing trusting relationships with them. She learned and used the jargon of HugePills Pharmaceuticals. She identified the key operational processes where she would begin to make changes gradually and with her team's participation.

At first, other managers resisted Joyce's proposals and refused to follow the new procedures that she implemented, but, gradually they began to see the benefits. Even the results of the annual employee engagement survey showed improvements. Eventually, other department managers began to look at their own operational processes and procedures, thus contributing to increase overall plant efficiency.

Joyce's example illustrates how individuals and organizational culture influence each other. Although Joyce was initially an external entity to Huge-Pills Pharmaceuticals, similar changes can be driven by employees with longer tenure in organizations. Even though we have emphasized that an organization's culture has an impact on employee engagement, you as a manager can make a difference by capitalizing on individual differences and monitoring your own levels of engagement.

LISTEN UP!

It's all about effectiveness and congruence.

Individual Differences Within an Organization's Culture

Factors such as generation, gender, education, socioeconomic status, previous experience, industry, organizational level, organizational role, geographic region, family size, and community involvement, among others, may lessen or increase the effect of organizational culture. Thus, individuals will respond differently to similar components of the culture and these components may have contrasting weights on their levels of engagement. Let's look at the stories of Jaleel and Trish who are peers at ReadyToRumble to illustrate some of these differences and what they can mean for you as a manager as you promote employee engagement.

Jaleel started working at ReadyTwoRumble as an intern in college, obtained an entry-level position, worked for three years in one department, and recently joined the shipping department to work on a project. Jaleel's entire career has been at ReadyTwoRumble and he is very loyal to the organization for what it has given him throughout the years. Jaleel speaks highly of ReadyTwoRumble wherever he has an opportunity to do so and encourages others to seek employment there. He is used to working long hours because their systems are at the top of their capacity and generating reports for senior management can take a lot of time; his family is used to his absence. Jaleel intends to continue working at ReadyTwoRumble until his retirement.

Trish worked in three other organizations before joining ReadyTwo-Rumble. She completed an internship as an exchange student in Japan, where she learned to speak Japanese. She then obtained an entry-level position and soon after became a team leader. ReadyTwoRumble recruited Trish because of her contributions and expertise. Until Trish started at ReadyTwoRumble, she only worked long hours when it was absolutely necessary because time with her family is very important to her. She is very technology savvy and uses it to maintain her productivity at very high levels, but the systems available at ReadyTwoRumble are becoming an obstacle in her performance. Trish is disappointed with the company and regrets not having asked more questions about technology and other resources before accepting their offer; she is already looking for another opportunity elsewhere.

Jaleel and Trish work at the same company and are subject to the effects of its culture. However, because of the differences in their backgrounds, the impact of a single element—the availability of technology—has a dissimilar consequence on each one of them. What is "business as usual" for Jaleel is totally unacceptable for Trish; therefore, their levels of engagement are totally opposite because of the "I" element. If you were their manager, you would need to work with those differences to help Jaleel to maintain his high levels of engagement and to find a way to increase Trish's level of engagement.

LISTEN UP!
Consider the individual when working with differences.

Now it's your turn.

Let's look at individual differences in your team.

1. Which individual differences are present in your team?

    _____

    _____

    _____

    _____

    _____

2. How are these individual differences having an impact on your employees' engagement?

    _____

    _____

    _____

    _____

3. What are you doing to address those differences to increase employee engagement?

    _____

    _____

    _____

Role of the Manager in the Organization's Culture

As a manager, you embody your company's culture for your employees, as they will interpret everything that you do and communicate as representative of your company and of its ways of working. You continuously contribute to shape that culture, as well as employee engagement, along with other levels of management in your company. You are uniquely positioned to either maintain your organization's culture or to begin to change it, because, whether you intend to or not, you lead by example.

Based on our experience working with clients from different industries, we propose that you could be a company's culture **Bodyguard**, **Steady One**, or **Transformer**. Let's look at how each one functions within a company's culture and how they contribute to foster employee engagement within that role.

» The **Bodyguard** is absolutely convinced that the company's culture is perfect as it is and proudly displays symbols of the company on clothing (for example, wearing a company pin) and in workspace (such as through pictures with senior management). The Bodyguard constantly reinforces the way to do business at the company to new employees at all levels, announcing her multiple years of service at every possible opportunity. The Bodyguard is often someone known and admired across organizational levels. Typically, the Bodyguard has held different positions of increasing responsibility over time and cannot even imagine what it would be like to work elsewhere. The Bodyguard defends the company vehemently from any perceived or real attack coming from an outsider or from a new employee. She strives to maintain the company's culture at all costs, and sometimes misses opportunities to innovate and make things better because of an unspoken fear of losing control. The Bodyguard promotes employee engagement through heightening organizational brand and image as well as through consistent communication. She may use performance management to perpetuate those employee behaviors that she believes to be appropriate for the company and extinguish those behaviors that she does not approve, thus, perhaps inadvertently, engendering polar opposites of employee engagement within the team.

» The **Steady One** understands the company's culture. He flows with changes over time, but very slowly. The Steady One may or may not have had experiences in other companies, but has stayed in the current one longer than the average manager. The Steady One has a long-term perspective on how the culture could be, but will not take any radical steps in that direction. Instead, he analyzes any project for its potential impact before deciding to support it and does so only if there is a very high degree of certainty for its success. The Steady One only supports employee initiatives that have undergone intensive scrutiny to minimize risk of failure for the employee as well as for himself. Even though the Steady One is a good source of information about the company's history and culture, his input is rarely sought. The Steady One hopes to stay in his current company until the end of his career and fears obsolescence if the culture changes dramatically. The Steady One promotes employee engagement through consistent communication that heighten the importance of careful analysis before taking action. He will pay considerable attention to detail during all activities related to performance management and will be very cautious when considering career opportunities for team members. In the end, the impact of the Steady One on employee engagement will also depend on the natural predisposition of the members of the team.

» The **Transformer** has a thorough understanding of the company's culture, but is able to look at it critically to identify what can be done better. Like the Bodyguard, the Transformer proudly displays symbols of the company and defends it, but the Transformer is very careful about not conveying fanaticism in expressions of loyalty because he knows that eventually he will go somewhere else to work. The Transformer is well known throughout the company, but has also held different positions in other companies. Others seek his opinions because they tend to be based on facts and trends instead of emotions; he is not blind to the shortcomings of the company's culture. The Transformer looks for information about best practices in other organizations and finds ways to adapt them so that they can be implemented quickly in his. The Transformer supports employee efforts to create and innovate within the boundaries of the company, even when doing so may mean tolerating and correcting mistakes. He empowers employees to make decisions, take risks, and make a difference. The Transformer encourages employee engagement mainly through leadership and communication as well as performance management, assuming responsibility for every outcome and supporting his employees in their journey.

Every organization needs Bodyguards, Steady Ones, and Transformers because they meet different needs at different moments in time. However, companies may tend to favor one over the other depending on what they do and how they do it. For example, you may find more Bodyguards in conservative industries such as banking and finance. In contrast, high-technology companies may have greater numbers of Transformers because they thrive on change and innovation.

Although we have presented the Bodyguard, Steady One, and Transformer of organizational culture from a manager's perspective, you may find variations of these three personas among the members of your team. We invite you to see how your persona is similar or different from that of the other members of your team.

A manager usually leads a team that already exists. If this is your situation, you will be addressing the needs of each member of your team to promote their engagement and, as you will see in other chapters of this book, you will need to consider where they are in their engagement process in your company and in their careers overall. However, you may participate in the recruitment and selection of new employees for your team or company. Because this process is the foundation for the company's culture of the future, we encourage you to take advantage of the opportunity to make a difference and "interview for engagement," asking questions about likes and dislikes as well as competencies. You will look for evidence of a positive predisposition toward the workplace in these interviews, which will only be the first step in the process of establishing that strong emotional connection necessary for an employee to become highly engaged.

In another chapter we describe a series of typical steps in the employee engagement process within a company. Before we close this chapter, we would like you to think about what we discussed in this last section.

Now it's your turn.

1. What do you think that the Bodyguard, Steady One, and Transformer personas can contribute to the culture of your workplace?

_____

_____

_____

2. How does each one contribute to the success of your team?

_____

_____

_____

3. Which one of the three personas resembles mostly how you are currently contributing to the culture of your workplace? Why?

_____

_____

_____

4. What cultural needs have not been met by the Bodyguard, the Steady One, and the Transformer?

_____

_____

_____

5. What can you do to address those needs?

_____

_____

_____

KEY POINTS AND TAKEAWAYS

- Organizational culture encompasses attitudes, beliefs, expectations, knowledge, language, opportunities, structure, and materials.
- Beliefs are internal representations of events.
- Attitudes play a critical role in employee engagement; they include emotional, behavioral, and cognitive components.
- Values embody what is not negotiable for the company.
- Employees bring values and beliefs into their workplaces.
- Expectations are part of the psychological contract.
- Those unwritten rules that are indispensable for success are part of knowledge.
- Take verbal and nonverbal language into consideration in communication.
- Opportunities are often included in the engagement equation.
- Structure influences how employees interact.
- Be aware of the resources needed.
- Bodyguard, Steady One, and Transformer—you need all three of them.

PART II

The Process of Employee Engagement and Its Steps: Engagement "I" Path

Introduction

Employee engagement is a process. In the next few chapters, we present its steps so that you can identify where your employees are in this process. The results of your assessment will help you to continue planning what you will do to promote employee engagement in your team. We begin our discussion of each step with a general overview. We also link the engagement drivers that we discussed in chapter 1 to each step. Later, we give you examples of typical employee behaviors in that step. Further, we recommend actions for you as a manager to take and to avoid; in other words, "dos and don'ts" for you to target the needs of your employees in that step. As you have seen so far in this book, each section contains questions for you to think about so that you can continue to apply what you have learned to your particular situation.

Before we start, here is something to consider: How engaged and in which step your employees are may be related to where they are in their careers and personal circumstances.

Engagement "I" Path

Our employee engagement model is called Engagement "I" Path. At first, you may think that we are suggesting that all employees go through all the steps in the same sequence. You may even think that we are contradicting ourselves after emphasizing the role of individual differences in engagement in other sections of this book. To clarify this important point, we are proposing a process model because it allows us to organize what happens in each step and to show how an employee goes from one step to the next one. Based on our research and our work, in many instances employees do go through steps in a particular order and then start all over again. However, as we have said before, each employee is different and we encourage you to pay attention to those differences. Moreover, in many cases, how an employee progresses from one step to the next will depend on what happens at a particular step, among other factors. As a manager, your job is to optimize that uniqueness to maximize employee engagement, acknowledging that some factors that affect employee engagement are outside of your span of control.

Figure 1 depicts the process that we propose: The process begins when the employee joins the organization in the Starting Out step, which usually lasts throughout the first six months of employment. As she learns her way

Figure 1   Employee Engagement "I" Path

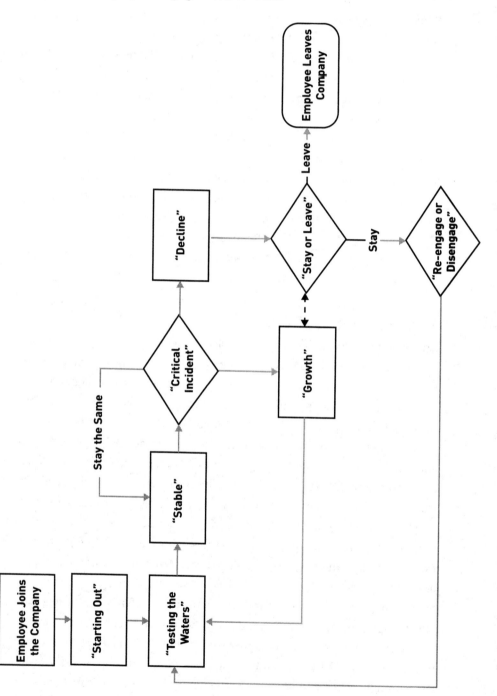

around the company, the employee enters the Testing the Waters step, which may extend until the first anniversary in the company. As she becomes more comfortable in the workplace, she enters the Stable step, and may stay there for a long time. If during the Stable step the employee goes through a Critical Incident, this could affect the employee's next move. She may return to the Stable step if her engagement is not affected by the Critical Incident, and then move to the Growth step. The employee who is in the Growth step may debate whether to Stay or Leave, or continue back to the Testing the Waters step, continuing the process from there. Although this may seem counterintuitive at first, the employee's experience every time that she moves forward will be comparable to starting something new all over again, therefore, she will need to find out if she made the right choices and if she is receiving what she expects before continuing moving along the Engagement "I" Path. In other words, she needs to step back to jump forward.

Alternatively, if the Critical Incident negatively affects the employee's engagement, she may enter the Decline step. If the employee enters the Decline step, she will choose whether to Stay or Leave. If she decides to Stay, she will enter the Re-engage or Disengage turning point and will return to the Testing the Waters step. Every time that an employee moves to a new step, she goes through a "reality check" of her new circumstances because, for her, the world changed and only by Testing the Waters will she know what is going on. If she decides to Leave, she could do so mentally, physically, or both, and her progression through the Engagement "I" Path will end.

We will now look at each one of these steps in detail. Chapter 3 will cover Starting Out and Testing the Waters, followed by chapter 4, which takes us into the Stable step as well as the Critical Incident. In chapter 5 we'll cover the options of Growth versus Decline, and chapter 6 wraps up the process with Stay or Leave and Re-engage or Disengage. At the end of the description of the entire process, we will cover the Key Points and Takeaways.

LISTEN UP!

When your mindset changes, your engagement changes.

CHAPTER 3:

Starting Out and Testing the Waters

Starting Out

Overview

This step is your golden opportunity as a manager to promote employee engagement because everything is new for the employee. He is hopeful, enthusiastic, and motivated about his new role and about the future. Similarly, you as a manager are confident about the employee's role in the company and his potential contributions. The team members are also expectant about the opportunity to share the work with a new member; however, they are more cautious in their approach. Those first experiences of the new employee with the company, with the team, and with you are crucial because they alter the new employee's perceptions about the workplace. What happens in this step will contribute to the employee's level of engagement throughout his tenure at your company.

LISTEN UP!

Capitalize on the silent language of first impressions.

Now it's your turn.

We would like you to begin to identify which step of the Engagement "I" Path employees are in. Who is in the Starting Out step? List the names of those employees in Worksheet 3.1.

Worksheet 3.1 Employees in the Starting Out Step

	EMPLOYEE NAMES
STARTING OUT	

We will now take a closer look at those engagement drivers that we introduced in chapter 1 and propose which ones are particularly important at this step.

Drivers

One of the drivers that we already discussed is organizational branding and image; it is important even before the employee joins the company because it is often what draws an employee to seek a position in that company. Base pay and incentive pay as well as overall benefits and flexible arrangements are part of the employment offer and together, they may persuade an employee to join a company. Total rewards, defined elsewhere in this book, will also play a key role in an employee's decision.

Once the employee begins the Starting Out step, other drivers such as performance management, particularly objectives, communication, recognition, and autonomy will have some bearing on employee engagement as the new employee navigates around the organization. Likewise, organizational management in general will inspire the new employee to form those important bonds with the company, the manager, and the team, which will serve to anchor the emotional components of engagement. Finally, even though this step typically only includes the first six months of employment, the new employee will begin to gather information about career opportunities and potential; their availability will alter those initial perceptions as the new employee confirms the appropriateness of the decision to be part of the company.

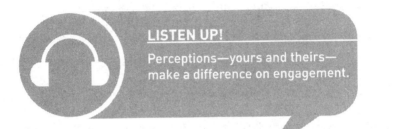

LISTEN UP!

Perceptions—yours and theirs—make a difference on engagement.

We will now share with you some examples of employee behaviors that you may notice during the Starting Out step related to employee level of engagement and ask you to identify who is displaying them.

Employee Behaviors

These are some employee behaviors that you may observe during the Starting Out step.

» Observes how others behave to learn the unspoken codes of the workplace about issues such as bureaucracy, rules, regulations, rewards, and taboos.

» Obtains information about tasks and responsibilities as well as about goals and objectives.

» Establishes and executes work habits and routines.

» Seeks to establish relationships with others in the division and outside of it.

» Looks for similarities and differences between herself and others, including the manager.

» Identifies sources of information and support.

» Speaks highly about the company and team in social media and elsewhere.

» Begins to wear and display company logos and other symbols.

» Participates eagerly in the onboarding process to learn about the company.

» Validates if the organization's values match his values.

» Pays attention to how leaders, particularly managers, communicate at all levels.

Now it's your turn.

Select which behaviors from this list you have noticed among the employees who are in the Starting Out Step, using Worksheet 3.2.

Worksheet 3.2   **Behaviors Observed From Employees in Starting Out Step**

BEHAVIORS	EMPLOYEE NAMES		
Observes how others behave to learn the unspoken codes of the workplace about issues such as bureaucracy, rules, regulations, rewards, and taboos.			
Obtains information about tasks and responsibilities as well as about goals and objectives.			
Establishes and executes work habits and routines.			
Seeks to establish relationships with others in the division and outside of it.			
Looks for similarities and differences between herself and others, including the manager.			
Identifies sources of information and support.			
Speaks highly about the company and team in social media and elsewhere.			
Begins to wear and display company logos and other symbols.			

BEHAVIORS	EMPLOYEE NAMES		
Participates eagerly in the onboarding process to learn about the company.			
Validates if the organization's values match his values.			
Pays attention to how leaders, particularly managers, communicate at all levels.			

Manager Dos and Don'ts

Here are some examples of what you should and should not do when an employee is in the Starting Out step. We acknowledge that this list is extensive because of the importance of this step in the employee's Engagement "I" Path. Please note that these dos and don'ts are not in any particular order.

Dos

»   Ensure that basic equipment, tools, and resources are available prior to the new employee's arrival.

»   Meet with the team before the new employee arrives to prepare the team to welcome the new member.

»   Introduce her to the team and others in the company promptly.

»   Welcome the new employee personally.

»   Provide information about the company, the job, and the team (onboarding).

»   Prepare additional targeted onboarding activities to facilitate the new employee's integration to the team.

»   Model appropriate behaviors in the company (dress code, speech, ways of address, communication style, work ethic, traditions).

»   Anticipate and remove barriers for employee's success.

»   Address issues with candor such as rumors, industry trends, reorganizations, promotions, and demotions, among others.

»   Help the employee to understand business goals and the big picture as well as her contribution to the company's bottom line.

» Specify and clarify roles, responsibilities, and expectations about yourself, the employee, the team, and others.

» Establish communication channels and frequency.

» Facilitate interactions with other departments and management.

» Provide timely and useful positive and developmental feedback.

» Respect the employee's need for privacy by avoiding personal questions.

» Encourage questions and experimentation from the employee.

» Create a "safe environment."

Don'ts

» Delay introductions to the team and to other members of the company.

» Procrastinate requesting basic equipment, tools, and resources for the new employee.

» Delegate welcoming and introducing the employee to another manager and department.

» Limit access of the employee to basic information about the company, the job, and the team.

» Demonstrate behaviors that are not consistent with the organizational image, values, and principles.

» Limit the onboarding process to what the company offers.

» Refuse to acknowledge and address issues such as rumors, industry trends, reorganizations, promotions, and demotions, among others.

» Leave expectations about the employee's work undefined.

» Refuse to give clues and suggestions about what the employee should be doing in terms of integrating into the company.

» Point out cultural mistakes that resulted from not having the appropriate information beforehand.

» Delay answering questions promptly and with not enough information.

» Criticize in public.

» Provide double messages (for example, encourage experimentation, but penalize for mistakes).

» Show favoritism in the team.

» Take questions personally.

» Be too personal.

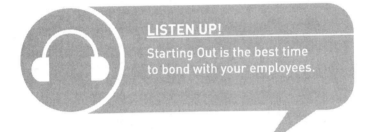

LISTEN UP!
Starting Out is the best time to bond with your employees.

Now it's your turn.

Worksheet 3.3 presents a behavior self-assessment for you to identify those behaviors that you have displayed or that you display typically. Place a check mark on the right column to indicate if you display those behaviors, you do not display them, or you display them sometimes.

Worksheet 3.3 Manager Behavior Self-Assessment: Starting Out Step

BEHAVIOR	YES	NO	SOMETIMES
DOS:			
Ensure that basic equipment, tools, and resources are available prior to the new employee's arrival.			

BEHAVIOR	YES	NO	SOMETIMES
Meet with the team before the new employee arrives to prepare the team to welcome the new member.			
Introduce her to the team and others in the company promptly.			
Welcome the new employee personally.			
Provide information about the company, the job, and the team (onboarding).			
Prepare additional targeted onboarding activities to facilitate the new employee's integration to the team.			
Model appropriate behaviors in the company (dress code, speech, ways of address, communication style, work ethic, traditions).			
Anticipate and remove barriers for employee's success.			
Address issues with candor such as rumors, industry trends, reorganizations, promotions, and demotions, among others.			
Help the employee to understand business goals and the big picture as well as her contribution to the company's bottom line.			
Specify and clarify roles, responsibilities, and expectations about yourself, the employee, the team, and others.			
Establish communication channels and frequency.			
Facilitate interactions with other departments and management.			
Provide timely and useful positive and developmental feedback.			
Respect the employee's need for privacy by avoiding personal questions.			
Encourage questions and experimentation from the employee.			

BEHAVIOR	YES	NO	SOMETIMES
Create a "safe environment."			
DON'TS:			
Delay introductions to the team and to other members of the company.			
Procrastinate requesting basic equipment, tools, and resources for the new employee.			
Delegate welcoming and introducing the employee to another manager and department.			
Limit access of the employee to basic information about the company, the job, and the team.			
Demonstrate behaviors that are not consistent with the organizational image, values, and principles.			
Limit the onboarding process to what the company offers.			
Refuse to acknowledge and address issues such as rumors, industry trends, reorganizations, promotions, and demotions, among others.			
Leave expectations about the employee's work undefined.			
Refuse to give clues and suggestions about what the employee should be doing in terms of integrating into the company.			
Point out cultural mistakes that resulted from not having the appropriate information beforehand.			
Delay answering questions promptly and with not enough information.			
Criticize in public.			
Provide double messages (for example, encourage experimentation, but penalize for mistakes).			

BEHAVIOR	YES	NO	SOMETIMES
Show favoritism in the team.			
Take questions personally.			
Be too personal.			

1. How many are dos and how many are don'ts?

2. Identify the three don'ts that you would like to turn into dos.

3. Identify the behaviors that you do sometimes and explain why you do so.

Testing the Waters

Overview

This step is your opportunity to continue to increase the engagement of that employee who has been a member of your team for the last six months. At this time, the employee validates if the decision to join the company was correct based on how well he fits with the company and its values. Questions such as, "Is this the right place for me?" "Is this place for real?" "What happened to the promises?" or "Where's the gold?" will be in the employee's mind as he seeks information. At the same time, you as a manager will be looking for signals that you made the correct decision to bring this employee into the company. By now, you have had some time to evaluate his capacity to contribute, adapt, and adjust to the team through the results that you have begun to see.

Now it's your turn.

Who is in the Testing the Waters step? List the names of those employees who are at this step in Worksheet 3.4.

Worksheet 3.4   Employees in the Testing the Waters Step

	EMPLOYEE NAMES
TESTING THE WATERS	

Drivers

At this step, the focus is less on image and more on alignment as the employee assesses how she fits in the new setting. The meaning of total rewards changes as she becomes more familiar with the new workplace and obtains firsthand information about those rewards. In this step, since the initial onboarding process has ended, the employee begins to experience the type of work and the size of the workload and can reach conclusions about the existent level of autonomy on the job. As she executes and completes tasks, she gets a sense of competence and progress as she finds meaning in the work (that is, intrinsic motivation). She gains insights into the flexibility of work arrangements, issues entailing work-life balance, and workplace stress through the communication and behaviors of the organization's leaders, particularly in terms of performance management. The respect and quality of co-workers gains sizeable importance as the employee interacts more closely with them and continues to seek information about the workplace and those unwritten rules that must be followed for success. In many instances, the employee looks for an environment conducive to good service to others. Potential career opportunities are a significant issue in the Testing the Waters step as the employee obtains information about what could be available for her in the future.

Following are some examples of employee behaviors that you may notice during the Testing the Waters step that relate to employee level of engagement. Then we'll ask you to identify who is displaying them.

Employee Behaviors

These are some employee behaviors that you may observe during the Testing the Waters step.

» Seeks additional assignments and challenges to demonstrate skills.

» Seeks reasons to work beyond external rewards.

» Completes tasks and tests the system to find out what can and cannot be done.

» Evaluates how much autonomy and flexibility is available to complete tasks.

» Delves into the relationship with the team.

» Assesses the quality of the interactions and calibrates how much he can trust others.

» Searches for opportunities to expand her internal network.

» Demonstrates that he is beginning to form a more realistic opinion of the company's or division's virtues and areas of opportunity.

» Detects inconsistencies between what the company presents to outsiders and what the company is really about; evaluates brand alignment.

» Asks a lot of questions.

» Compares the type of work, size of workload, and classes of rewards available to different team members.

» Incorporates suggestions into her work.

» Searches for opportunities to begin to contribute and for ways those contributions can noticed and acknowledged.

LISTEN UP!
Is this the best place for me?
A "yes" is up to you.

Now it's your turn.

Select which behaviors from this list you have noticed among the employees who are in the Testing the Waters step in Worksheet 3.5.

Worksheet 3.5 Behaviors Observed From Employees in the Testing the Waters Step

BEHAVIORS	EMPLOYEE NAMES			
Seeks additional assignments and challenges to demonstrate skills.				
Seeks reasons to work beyond external rewards.				
Completes tasks and tests the system to find out what can and cannot be done.				
Evaluates how much autonomy and flexibility is available to complete tasks.				
Delves into the relationship with the team.				
Assesses the quality of the interactions and calibrates how much he can trust others.				
Searches for opportunities to expand her internal network.				
Demonstrates that he is beginning to form a more realistic opinion of the company's or division's virtues and areas of opportunity.				

BEHAVIORS	EMPLOYEE NAMES		
Detects inconsistencies between what the company presents to outsiders and what the company is really about; evaluates brand alignment.			
Asks a lot of questions.			
Compares the type of work, size of workload, and classes of rewards available to different team members.			
Incorporates suggestions into her work.			
Searches for opportunities to begin to contribute and for ways those contributions can be noticed and acknowledged.			

Manager Dos and Don'ts

Now that you are more familiar with your employee's experience during the Testing the Waters step, we suggest some actions for you to take and avoid to promote employee engagement during this step. As before, please note that these dos and don'ts are not in any particular order.

Dos

- » Coach the employee on how to approach different situations.
- » Answer questions and allow experimentation from the employee.
- » Create a "safe environment" to stretch talents and make mistakes.
- » Conduct "reality checks" for expectations, role, and career.
- » Communicate, communicate, communicate.
- » Avoid criticism and sarcasm.
- » Model appropriate behaviors in the company (dress code, speech, ways of address, communication style, work ethic, traditions).
- » Anticipate barriers for the employee's success.
- » Provide timely and useful positive and developmental feedback.
- » Handle performance issues fairly and equitably (workload, work-life balance, performance management).
- » Be fair and honest.

Don'ts

» Miss opportunities to coach the employee on important issues or assignments.

» Minimize the importance of the employee for the company and the team.

» Show favoritism in the team.

» Be secretive about information that can be shared.

» React to problems instead of anticipating them.

» Only point out mistakes and faults.

» Ignore positive or appropriate actions and behaviors.

» Delay positive and developmental feedback until formal performance reviews.

» Wait for the employee to make mistakes that could have been avoided and then reprimand the employee for those mistakes.

Now it's your turn.

Worksheet 3.6 presents a behavior self-assessment for you to identify those behaviors that you have displayed or that you display typically. Place a check mark on the right column to indicate if you display those behaviors, you do not display them, or you display them sometimes.

Worksheet 3.6   Manager Behavior Self-Assessment: Testing the Waters Step

BEHAVIOR	YES	NO	SOMETIMES
DOS:			
Coach the employee on how to approach different situations.			
Answer questions and encourage experimentation from the employee.			

BEHAVIOR	YES	NO	SOMETIMES
Create a "safe environment" to stretch talents and make mistakes.			
Conduct "reality checks" for expectations, role, and career.			
Communicate, communicate, communicate.			
Avoid criticism and sarcasm.			
Model appropriate behaviors in the company (dress code, speech, ways of address, communication style, work ethic, traditions).			
Anticipate barriers for the employee's success.			
Provide timely and useful positive and developmental feedback.			
Handle performance issues fairly and equitably (workload, work-life balance, performance management).			
Be fair and honest.			
DON'TS:			
Miss opportunities to coach the employee on important issues or assignments.			
Minimize the importance of the employee for the company and the team.			
Show favoritism in the team.			
Be secretive about information that can be shared.			
React to problems instead of anticipating them.			
Only point out mistakes and faults.			
Ignore positive or appropriate actions and behaviors.			

BEHAVIOR	YES	NO	SOMETIMES
Delay positive and developmental feedback until formal performance reviews.			
Wait for the employee to make mistakes that could have been avoided and then reprimand the employee for those mistakes.			

1. How many are dos and how many are don'ts?

    _____

    _____

    _____

2. Identify the three don'ts that you would like to turn into dos.

    _____

    _____

    _____

3. Identify the behaviors that you do sometimes and explain why you do so.

    _____

    _____

    _____

In the next chapter we will explore the next two steps in the Engagement "I" Path: the Stable step, and the Critical Incident step.

CHAPTER 4:

Stable and Critical Incident

Stable

Overview

As the word stable indicates, when the employee reaches this step, he is convinced that the company is the right place for him to be at that time. This step is your opportunity to continue to promote, reinforce, and increase employee engagement. Therefore, your role as a manager acquires additional importance because you must strive to—at a minimum—maintain the current level of employee engagement.

Now it's your turn.

Who is in the Stable step? List the names of those employees in Worksheet 4.1.

Worksheet 4.1   **Employees in the Stable Step**

	EMPLOYEE NAMES
STABLE	

Drivers

The overall atmosphere and environment in the workplace is very important at this step because the employee has made a decision to stay and this is where she will spend most of her time. Therefore, she must feel comfortable in the setting and with her team and management. Generally, employees prefer environments where they feel safe and secure. For many employees, total rewards available will figure prominently in this step because they represent solidness in the company; for them, any changes may be an indicator of impending unwelcome variations in the current situation, which could disturb the obtained level of stability. For others, potential career and promotion opportunities may be more meaningful as they envision a future in the company and try to define that future and picture what professional growth will look like.

Management and performance issues gain an additional and different significance in this step. Many employees have already formed a firm opinion of the company's management and have set up expectations. Manager communication, particularly under any conditions of uncertainty, will continue to influence employee engagement either positively or negatively. Performance management issues are tied directly to management issues at this step because employees understand that management (you are part of it) ultimately decides the policy for them. Let's see an example.

Management establishes goals and objectives and determines when to communicate them to employees. Management also sets up performance management systems and metrics under which the employee's results and achievement will be appraised. Management makes decisions about resource availability and distribution to meet goals and objectives. In addition, management models expectations about work-life balance and stress management which, because of their long-term importance for the employee, will be critical in this step.

Employee Behaviors

These are some employee behaviors that you may observe during the Stable step of the Engagement "I" Path.

» Plays it "safe" because this is the place where she intends to stay.

» Looks for information about career opportunities inside the company and seeks answers to the question, "What kind of future will I have here?"

» Sees negative and positive experiences as opportunities to learn.

» Minimizes the impact of negative experiences. For example: "I take glitches as they come along, but shrug them off."

» Speaks highly about the company in social media and elsewhere with conviction.

» Provides specific examples of brand alignment based on personal experience.

» Accepts the organization as it is, including its virtues and areas of opportunity.

» Models teamwork.

» Defends the company when she perceives it to be under a threat of any kind. For example: "I fully support this place regardless of what anyone says."

» Goes out of his way to serve customers whether it is part of the job or not.

Now it's your turn.

Select which behaviors from this list you have noticed among the employees who are in the Stable step in Worksheet 4.2.

Worksheet 4.2 Behaviors Observed From Employees in Stable Step

BEHAVIORS	EMPLOYEE NAMES		
Plays it "safe" because this is the place where she intends to stay.			
Looks for information about career opportunities inside the company and seeks answers to the question, "What kind of future will I have here?"			

BEHAVIORS	EMPLOYEE NAMES		
Sees negative and positive experiences as opportunities to learn.			
Minimizes the impact of negative experiences. For example: "I take glitches as they come along, but shrug them off."			
Speaks highly about the company in social media and elsewhere with conviction.			
Provides specific examples of brand alignment based on personal experience.			
Accepts the company as it is, including its virtues and areas of opportunity.			
Models teamwork.			
Defends the company when she perceives it to be under a threat of any kind. For example: "I fully support this place regardless of what anyone says."			
Goes out of his way to serve customers whether it is part of the job or not.			

Manager Dos and Don'ts

In this section we present some examples of what you should and should not do when an employee is in the Stable step. We are not presenting them in any particular order of importance.

Dos

» Provide timely and useful positive and developmental feedback.

» Encourage questions and experimentation from the employee.

» Avoid miscommunication.

» Create a safe environment to stretch talents and make mistakes.

» Conduct reality checks for expectations about role, company, and career.

» Appreciate and value diversity in the team (age, gender, education, experience).

» Look for evidence of engagement or for risk of disengagement.

» Anticipate and remove barriers for employee's success.

» Be consistent in your messages to the employee (for example, what is important and why).

» Handle performance issues fairly and equitably (workload, work-life balance, performance management).

» Focus your attention on the employee and reject interruptions during meetings with the employee.

» Solve and anticipate problems.

Don'ts

» Only point out mistakes and faults.

» Ignore positive or appropriate actions and behaviors.

» Delay positive and developmental feedback until performance reviews.

» Limit opportunities for employee development and growth.

» Assign lackluster projects.

» Be secretive about information that can be shared.

» Overlook initial signals and behaviors of employee disengagement and postpone addressing signals and behaviors of employee disengagement.

» Wait for the employee to make mistakes that could have been avoided and then reprimand him for those mistakes.

» Delay responding or returning calls to the employee.

» Delegate a role without delegating the authority.

LISTEN UP!

Create and maintain a sense of safety.

Now it's your turn.

Worksheet 4.3 presents a behavior self-assessment for you to identify those behaviors that you have displayed or that you display typically. Place a check mark on the right column to indicate if you display those behaviors, you do not display them, or you display them sometimes.

Worksheet 4.3   Manager Behavior Self-Assessment: Stable Step

BEHAVIOR	YES	NO	SOMETIMES
DOS:			
Provide timely and useful positive and developmental feedback.			
Encourage questions and experimentation from the employee.			
Avoid miscommunication.			
Create a safe environment to stretch talents and make mistakes.			
Conduct reality checks for expectations about role, company, and career.			
Appreciate and value diversity in the team (age, gender, experience).			
Look for evidence of engagement or for risk of disengagement.			

BEHAVIOR	YES	NO	SOMETIMES
Anticipate and remove barriers for employee's success.			
Be consistent in your messages to the employee (for example, what is important and why).			
Handle performance issues fairly and equitably (workload, work-life balance, performance management).			
Focus your attention on the employee and reject interruptions during meetings with the employee.			
Solve and anticipate problems.			
DON'TS:			
Only point out mistakes and faults.			
Ignore positive or appropriate actions and behaviors.			
Delay positive and developmental feedback until performance reviews.			
Limit opportunities for employee development and growth.			
Assign lackluster projects.			
Be secretive about information that can be shared.			
Overlook initial signals and behaviors of employee disengagement and postpone addressing signals and behaviors of employee disengagement.			
Wait for the employee to make mistakes that could have been avoided and then reprimand him for those mistakes.			
Delay responding or returning calls to the employee.			
Delegate a role without delegating the authority.			

1. How many are dos and how many are don'ts?

   _____

   _____

   _____

2. Identify the three don'ts that you would like to turn into dos.

   _____

   _____

   _____

3. Identify the behaviors that you do sometimes and explain why you do so.

   _____

   _____

   _____

Critical Incidents

Overview

Critical Incidents represent the greatest risk for rapid disengagement or increase in engagement because they entail a shift in the employee's relationship with the manager or company. A Critical Incident is a turning point that can determine the path that the employee will follow through the remaining steps of the Engagement "I" Path. Although the results of a Critical Incident will undoubtedly depend on how you (as a manager) and the company handle the incident, rest assured that other factors outside of your control, such as high-level decisions or past experiences, may affect those results. However, you can still influence those results regardless of your position and make a difference on how the employee reacts to the Critical Incident and the path that she follows afterward, either inside or outside of the organization.

Some possible Critical Incidents are: performance reviews, promotions and demotions, pay raises, incentive bonuses, interpersonal conflicts, development opportunities, role changes, priority changes, structure changes, work-life balance, resource availability, rewards distribution, policy changes, procedure changes, company mergers, company acquisitions, staff layoffs, business conditions, and business results. Elements external to the organization such as personal transitions, natural disasters, and economic conditions may serve to worsen or lessen the impact of Critical Incidents. Let's see an example of Critical Incidents for three employees.

Sarah has been selected to lead a strategic project (a development opportunity) and is very excited about it. She counts on the support of her immediate family to share domestic responsibilities so that she can focus on the project as necessary, but they are not helping.

Michelle was informed that she will begin to report to a different manager with whom she does not have a positive relationship (structure changes).

Phillip just received his performance review and learned that his assessment and his peer's assessment were very similar. Phillip is angry because he does not think that his peer's work is as good as his.

After a Critical Incident, an employee's engagement may go in one of three directions: stay the same, grow, or decline. We will discuss each one of these directions.

An employee's level of engagement may increase and continue increasing over time depending on his interpretation of dimensions of the Critical Incident, such as its relative importance for him and how he perceives that he and others were treated during the incident. For example, the Critical Incident may be related to something that seems to be minimally important, such as reassignments of workspaces in an office. For an employee who has always worked in cubicles, being assigned to another cubicle may have relatively minor importance compared to being assigned to work in an office for the first time. The level of engagement of the employee who has a new cubicle assignment may not increase significantly, thus staying the same, unless he is allowed to choose the cubicle or is given some flexibility about how to decorate the space among other possibilities. In contrast, the levels of engagement of the employee will, very likely, increase significantly if he is assigned to work in an office for the first time because of the benefits typically associated with private workspaces such as privacy and status. Whether the office has windows or not may have an additional impact on that employee's level of engagement.

Before we continue our discussion, we would like you to identify three employees in your team who have experienced Critical Incidents; your perceptions of their level of engagement before and after the incident; and whether their engagement stayed the same, increased, or decreased after the incident. We encourage you to consider any previous experiences of those employees that may have affected how they reacted to the Critical Incident.

Now it's your turn.

1. Complete the following table in Worksheet 4.4 to put together the information about your employees and their Critical Incidents. Include your perceptions about whether their engagement stayed the same, increased, or decreased after the Critical Incident under the column labeled Comments, as well as any possible impact of previous experiences on the resulting level of engagement.

Worksheet 4.4   Information About Employee Critical Incidents

EMPLOYEE NAME	CRITICAL INCIDENT	ENGAGEMENT BEFORE	ENGAGEMENT AFTER	COMMENTS

2. Describe a Critical Incident that you have experienced.

_____

_____

3. What was your engagement before and after the Critical Incident?

_____

_____

4. Did your engagement stay the same, increase, or decrease after the Critical Incident?

    _____

    _____

5. Why do you think that your engagement stayed the same, increased, or decreased after the Critical Incident?

    _____

    _____

Let's continue with our discussion of the drivers of employee engagement to see which ones are particularly important at the occurrence of a Critical Incident.

Drivers

The key to employee engagement during a Critical Incident is to anticipate the questions that the employee will raise whether she communicates them or not. By anticipating the employee's information needs, you as a manager will be ready to address any concerns that may have a pivotal role in the engagement path that the employee follows after the Critical Incident. Management is an important driver of employee engagement during a Critical Incident and its aftermath.

LISTEN UP!

A Critical Incident can be an opportunity in disguise.

Organizational image and brand alignment are important for the employee because she may find a disconnect between them depending on how the incident is handled. Let us look at an example.

YouWillBeHereForever prides itself as being a company that cares about the future of its employees. One Monday morning, all employees were requested to attend an informational meeting where they learned about changes to the pension plan that affected the time when many long-term employees would be leaving the company as retirees. Specifically, the benefits of the pension plan would not be available for employees who joined the company after a certain date and they would be frozen as of a particular date for the remaining employees. Thus, those employees who still would receive pensions would not accumulate additional benefits even though they still had to continue working until their required retirement age.

To anticipate emotional reactions to this Critical Incident, the management explained the rationale for the change, provided additional information about what benefits would remain effective, and answered questions from the audience.

Let's analyze what happened at this company:

» How do you think that the employees of YouWillBeHereForever would have reacted if, instead of being requested to attend a meeting where they could ask questions, they received a generic email informing them about the change?

» If the message was received via email, do you think they would have felt that YouWillBeHereForever really cared about them as employees?

» Do you think that their level of engagement would have increased, decreased, or remained stable after this Critical Incident if they had received the message via email?

In the example of the employees of YouWillBeHereForever, the engagement levels of those employees declined until they were able to "digest" the news. If you as a manager have to handle a situation such as the one at YouWillBeHereForever, you will need to work with each employee individually to help them to return to the Stable step because benefits are attached to the "I" (me).

Career opportunities and career potential are two areas that employees also pay attention to during a Critical Incident because they represent their future in a company. Let us look at an example.

A division of Indispensable, Inc. underwent its third management reorganization in three years as a result of turnover and shifts in customer preferences. In the last reorganization, Therese, a supervisor who was a direct report of the division's manager, became an individual contributor reporting to a former peer supervisor; her former direct reports became her peers and she lost the level of access to upper management that she had enjoyed until this change. As a result of this demotion, Therese perceived that her career opportunities at Indispensable, Inc. would be limited in the future. Do you think that Therese's level of engagement increased, decreased, or remained the same after this Critical Incident?

Performance management gains noteworthy significance because many Critical Incidents belong to this dimension of the workplace. Employees will be particularly sensitive to any perceptions of discrepancies in terms of how managers and other leaders handle its different components.

Topics related to total rewards, including base pay, incentive pay, and overall benefits will also be in the forefront of the employee's analysis of the Critical Incident and its consequences. Let's learn more about Therese's experience to illustrate what we mean.

When Therese was notified of the change in structure that would require her to be an individual contributor reporting to a former peer supervisor, she was informed that her total rewards would not change. This information provided her with some stability as she internalized the impact and consequences of this Critical Incident.

We will continue to share with you some examples of behaviors that you may notice among your employees. We will now focus on employee behaviors during and after a Critical Incident as related to employee level of engagement.

LISTEN UP!

Remember the importance of persuasion and influence after the Critical Incident.

Employee Behaviors

These are some employee behaviors that you may observe during and after a Critical Incident.

- » Assesses impact on present and future job prospects and career opportunities.

- » Seeks answers to questions such as: "Should I stay here?" "Will they keep me here?" "What can I do differently now and where can I do it?" "Is there something better for me elsewhere?"

- » Quality and quantity of tasks completed increase, decrease, or stay the same.

- » Questions motives of self and others involved in the incident especially if it is negative.

- » Seeks support from internal and external networks based on results of assessment of their quantity and quality.

- » Becomes reserved and withdrawn in interactions with others or overtly emotional depending on results of assessment of their quantity and quality.

- » Nature and quality of interactions changes. May seek more or less contact, be more or less superficial in casual contact, communicate for instrumental instead of social purposes, react more or less defensively to feedback, and assume a more or less aggressive stance with team.

- » If he perceives the Critical Incident as negative, may speak negatively, directly, or indirectly, about the company and the manager in social media.

- » Limits involvement in activities that typically entail contact with other levels of management to a minimum, such as holiday parties, while deciding what to do in response to the Critical Incident.

- » Reacts emotionally to Critical Incident either positively or negatively.

» Changes usual way to communicate relying more on written methods such as email to generate data and documentation about the incident.

» Talks a lot or not at all.

» Renegotiates the psychological contract.

Now it's your turn.

Select which behaviors from this list you have noticed among the employees who have experienced a Critical Incident in Worksheet 4.5.

Worksheet 4.5 Behaviors Observed From Employees Experiencing a Critical Incident

BEHAVIORS	EMPLOYEE NAMES		
Assesses impact on present and future job prospects and career opportunities.			
Seeks answers to questions such as: "Should I stay here?" "Will they keep me here?" "What can I do differently now and where can I do it?" "Is there something better for me elsewhere?"			
Quality and quantity of tasks completed increase, decrease, or stay the same.			
Questions motives of self and others involved in the incident especially if it is negative.			
Seeks support from internal and external networks based on results of assessment of their quantity and quality.			
Becomes reserved and withdrawn in interactions with others or overtly emotional depending on results of assessment of their quantity and quality.			
Nature and quality of interactions changes. May seek more or less contact, be more or less superficial in casual contact, communicate for instrumental instead of social purposes, react more or less defensively to feedback, and assume a more or less aggressive stance with team.			

BEHAVIORS	EMPLOYEE NAMES		
If he perceives the Critical Incident as negative, may speak negatively, directly or indirectly, about the company and the manager in social media and other outlets.			
Limits involvement in activities that typically entail contact with other levels of management to a minimum, such as holiday parties, while deciding what to do in response to the Critical Incident.			
Reacts emotionally to Critical Incident either positively or negatively.			
Changes usual way to communicate relying more on written methods such as email to generate data and documentation about the incident.			
Talks a lot or not at all.			
Renegotiates the psychological contract.			

Manager Dos and Don'ts

Here are some examples of what you should and should not do when an employee is experiencing a Critical Incident.

Dos

» Accept the incident and its outcomes or consequences.

» Reinforce positive behaviors and contributions, and correct what is inappropriate.

» Conduct reality checks for expectations about role, company, and career.

» Provide information to pertinent parties to minimize rumors and their impact.

» Anticipate and remove barriers for employee stability or for going back to the Stable step.

» Support questions from the employee.

» Be there.

» Handle performance issues such as workload, work-life balance, and performance management fairly and equitably.

» Provide dignified options to the employee.

» Offer available organizational resources to the employee.

» Accept vulnerability and deal with emotions.

Don'ts

» Promise what you cannot get or control.

» Point out only mistakes and faults.

» Create incorrect expectations about the employee's future in the company such as a promotion or increased likelihood of staying in the company in a case of "progressive discipline or else."

» Overlook signals and behaviors of employee disengagement.

» Be in an "emergency call mode" every day.

» Withhold information from the employee because she is not trustworthy.

» Show disrespect and disregard for the employee.

» Withhold organizational resources from the employee.

» Make unilateral decisions about the employee's future in the company whenever possible.

» Make references to previous situations at all times.

» Make comparisons.

LISTEN UP!
Don't push!

Now it's your turn.

Worksheet 4.6 presents a behavior self-assessment for you to identify those behaviors that you have displayed or that you display typically when an employee is experiencing a Critical Incident. Place a check mark on the right column to indicate if you display those behaviors, you do not display them, or you display them sometimes.

Worksheet 4.6   Manager Behavior Self-Assessment: Critical Incident Turning Point

BEHAVIOR	YES	NO	SOMETIMES
DOS:			
Accept the incident and its outcomes or consequences.			
Reinforce positive behaviors and contributions, and correct what is inappropriate.			
Conduct reality checks for expectations about role, company, and career.			
Provide information to pertinent parties to minimize rumors and their impact.			
Anticipate and remove barriers for employee stability or for going back to the Stable step.			
Support questions from the employee.			
Be there.			
Handle performance issues, such as workload, work-life balance, and performance management fairly and equitably.			
Provide dignified options to the employee.			
Offer available organizational resources to the employee.			
Accept vulnerability and deal with emotions.			

BEHAVIOR	YES	NO	SOMETIMES
DON'TS:			
Promise what you cannot get or control.			
Point out only mistakes and faults.			
Create incorrect expectations about the employee's future in the company such as a promotion or increased likelihood of staying in the company in a case of "progressive discipline or else."			
Overlook signals and behaviors of employee disengagement.			
Be in an "emergency call mode" every day.			
Withhold information from the employee because she is not trustworthy.			
Show disrespect and disregard for the employee.			
Withhold organizational resources from the employee.			
Make unilateral decisions about the employee's future in the company whenever possible.			
Make references to previous situations at all times.			
Make comparisons.			

1. How many are dos and how many are don'ts?

   _____

   _____

   _____

2. Identify the three don'ts that you would like to turn into dos.

   _____

   _____

   _____

3. Identify the behaviors that you do sometimes and explain why you do so.

_____

_____

_____

In the next chapter, we will explore the next step in the Engagement "I" Path: Growth and Decline.

CHAPTER 5:
Growth and Decline

Growth
Overview

This step is usually a direct result of a Critical Incident. An employee's level of engagement may increase (and continue increasing over time) depending on the Critical Incident. It's a step where the employee sees ample career development, lateral movements, role changes, function changes, knowledge acquisition, vertical movements, stretch assignments, special projects, job rotations, cross-training opportunities, and special assignments. After the employee's engagement begins to increase in the Growth step, she will return to the Testing the Waters step as she ascertains and redefines her relationship with the company, which was fortified by the lessons learned during the Critical Incident and its resolution.

Before we continue our discussion, we would like you to continue to identify in which step of the Engagement "I" Path your employees are.

Now it's your turn.

Who is in the Growth step? List the names of those employees who are in this step in Worksheet 5.1.

Worksheet 5.1   Employees in the Growth Step

	EMPLOYEE NAMES		
GROWTH			

Drivers

Employee perceptions of fairness and transparency during the Critical Incident will modify subsequent engagement levels. Management and performance management are the primary drivers of employee engagement that exert the most influence in the path that the employee will follow after a Critical Incident, under the Growth step. We will now look at each one of these drivers in the context of the Growth step.

How the company's management communicates information, provides resources, and models behavior will gain additional saliency for the employee to move to the Growth step. Employee engagement will grow when employees perceive that the management openly shares information, offers resources (such as financial planning or counseling services), and demonstrates empathy in interactions (for example, acknowledgment of employee's emotional displays).

In terms of performance management, engagement will grow as a result of employees' perceptions of fairness in performance reviews, development opportunities, and work allocation among other dimensions. Most importantly, employee engagement will grow as an outcome of explicit sensitivity, trust, and respect for the human side of the situation that became the Critical Incident. In return, employees will be more likely to go out of their way to do what is necessary to contribute to the common good.

LISTEN UP!

Be empathetic, sensitive, and respectful of your employees. It pays off.

We will continue to share with you some examples of behaviors that you may notice among your employees. We will now focus on employee behaviors during the Growth step that are related to employee level of engagement. At the end of the list, again we will ask you to identify who is displaying these behaviors.

Employee Behaviors

These are some employee behaviors that you may observe during the Growth step.

- » Shows minimal signs of stress.
- » Shows atypical punctuality in starting the workday or workweek.
- » Dedicates extraordinary efforts to tasks and projects.
- » Is willing to spend additional time on work-related activities during the workdays or weekends.
- » Increased work-related interactions with peers and managers.
- » Values safety and stability.
- » Participation in the office grapevine is constructive or minimal.
- » Shows overall positive attitude toward the company and the team.
- » Speaks positively about the company and growth opportunities.
- » Displays company and team logos and symbols with pride.
- » Participates in work-related after-hours events.
- » Quality of work improves.

Now it's your turn.

Select which behaviors from this list you have noticed among the employees who are in the Growth step in Worksheet 5.2.

Worksheet 5.2   Behaviors Observed From Employees in Growth Step

BEHAVIORS	EMPLOYEE NAMES		
Shows minimal signs of stress.			
Shows atypical punctuality in starting the workday or workweek.			
Dedicates extraordinary efforts to tasks and projects.			
Is willing to spend additional time on work-related activities during the workdays or weekends.			
Increased work-related interactions with peers and managers.			
Values safety and stability.			
Participation in the office grapevine is constructive or minimal.			
Shows overall positive attitude toward the company and the team.			
Speaks positively about the company and growth opportunities.			
Displays company and team logos and symbols with pride.			
Participates in work-related after-hours events.			
Quality of work improves.			

Manager Dos and Don'ts

Here are some examples of what you should and should not do when an employee is in the Growth step.

Dos

» Identify and provide stretch assignments.

» Share the employee's purpose.

» Involve the employee in decisions about how to complete tasks and provide general guidance to complete them.

» Allow employee autonomy in task-related decisions.

» Facilitate access to resources.

» Encourage interactions within the team and the formation of relationships outside of the team.

» Find opportunities for the employee to interact with other levels of the company.

» Seek ways for the employee to serve as spokesperson or representative of the company.

» Pay close attention to the employee's signals and behaviors of engagement or disengagement.

» Provide order and structure.

» Guide employees.

» Assign new responsibilities.

» Anticipate and remove barriers for employee performance.

» Allow communication.

» Offer available organizational resources to employee.

» Handle performance issues fairly and equitably (workload, work-life balance, performance management).

» Involve the employee in decisions about his future in the company.

Don'ts

» Only point out mistakes and faults.

» Create incorrect expectations about the employee's future in the company such as promotions or job security. Remember: not everyone gets every opportunity.

» Monitor every detail of the tasks as they are completed.

» Minimize importance of employee for the company and the team.

» Show favoritism in the team.

» Show disrespect and disregard for the employee.

» Limit employee participation in work-related activities.

» Be secretive about information that can be shared.

» Take advantage of the employee.

» Provide incorrect information.

» Withhold information and organizational resources from the employee.

» Demonstrate low levels of engagement.

» Ignore positive or appropriate actions and behaviors.

» Disregard opportunities to recognize the employee and take achievements for granted.

LISTEN UP!

Expect the best from your employees. Why not?

Now it's your turn.

Worksheet 5.3 presents a behavior self-assessment for you to identify those behaviors that you have displayed or that you display typically. Place a check mark on the right column to indicate if you display those behaviors, you do not display them, or you display them sometimes.

Worksheet 5.3   Manager Behavior Self-Assessment: Growth Step

BEHAVIOR	YES	NO	SOMETIMES
DOS:			
Identify and provide stretch assignments.			
Share the employee's purpose.			
Involve the employee in decisions about how to complete tasks and provide general guidance to complete them.			
Allow employee autonomy in task-related decisions.			
Facilitate access to resources.			
Encourage interactions within the team and encourage the formation of relationships outside of the team.			
Find opportunities for the employee to interact with other levels of the company.			
Seek ways for the employee to serve as spokesperson or representative of the company.			
Pay close attention to the employee's signals and behaviors of engagement or disengagement.			
Provide order and structure.			
Guide employees.			
Assign new responsibilities.			
Anticipate and remove barriers for employee performance.			
Allow communication.			
Offer available organizational resources to employee.			
Handle performance issues fairly and equitably (workload, work-life balance, performance management).			
Involve the employee in decisions about his future in the company.			

BEHAVIOR	YES	NO	SOMETIMES
DON'TS:			
Only point out mistakes and faults.			
Create incorrect expectations about the employee's future in the company such as promotions or job security. Remember: not everyone gets every opportunity.			
Monitor every detail of the tasks as they are completed.			
Minimize importance of employee for the company and the team.			
Show favoritism in the team.			
Show disrespect and disregard for the employee.			
Limit employee participation in work-related activities.			
Be secretive about information that can be shared.			
Take advantage of the employee.			
Provide incorrect information.			
Withhold information and organizational resources from the employee.			
Demonstrate low levels of engagement.			
Ignore positive or appropriate actions and behaviors.			
Disregard opportunities to recognize the employee and take achievements for granted.			

1.   How many are dos and how many are don'ts?

_____

_____

_____

_____

2. Identify the three don'ts that you would like to turn into dos.

    _____

    _____

    _____

    _____

3. Identify the behaviors that you do sometimes and explain why
    you do so.

    _____

    _____

    _____

    _____

Decline
Overview

This step is usually a direct result of a Critical Incident and represents the opposite behaviors of the step that we characterized as Growth. An employee's level of engagement may decrease (and continue decreasing over time) depending on his interpretation of the dimensions of the Critical Incident. In the example of the reassignments of workspace that we introduced in the discussion of the Critical Incident step, an employee who is assigned to work in a cubicle after working in an office may have a totally different perception of this Critical Incident than an employee who has always worked in cubicles. The employee who will not be working in an office any longer may perceive this change as a loss of privacy, status, and perks, and his levels of engagement will begin to decline.

Now it's your turn.

Who is in the Decline step? List the names of those employees who are in this step in Worksheet 5.4.

Worksheet 5.4   Employees in the Decline Step

	EMPLOYEE NAMES
DECLINE	

Drivers

The same primary drivers that influence Growth in engagement—namely, management and performance management—will modify subsequent employee engagement levels, but in the opposite direction. We will now look at management and performance management in the context of the Decline step. Employee engagement will decline when they perceive that the management does not share information, denies resources to employees (such as work-related Internet access), and shows inconsistency in behaviors (for example, does not provide napkins for employee coffee breaks but brings out the best china for executive coffee breaks).

In our example of the change in pension plans in YouWillBeHereForever, the engagement levels of the employees who would not be able to retire as planned declined; they believed they had dedicated many years of their lives to the company and expected to retire at a certain time and with a certain level of income, which now will not be there for them. Also, the engagement levels of other employees declined because they no longer believe they should devote years of their lives to an employer without any provisions for their future well-being.

Engagement will also decline when employees do not perceive equality and sensitivity in reward distribution, development opportunities, performance reviews, and flexible arrangements. In the Decline step, how employees see the team's high and low performers are managed will gain salience, particularly if high performers are assigned the tasks that low performers cannot complete successfully. By requiring additional work from high performers and reducing the workload of low performers, managers would be penalizing high performers and rewarding low performers. Thus, the engagement levels of high performers will begin to decline and other drivers of engagement, such as total rewards, would become a new source of concern for those employees.

LISTEN UP!

Take the time to ask yourself the question: Are your employees with you or against you?

We will again share with you some examples of behaviors that you may notice among your employees, focusing on those that occur during the Decline step that are related to employee level of engagement. At the end of the list, again we will ask you to identify who is displaying these behaviors as you continue your plans to increase employee engagement.

Employee Behaviors

These are some employee behaviors that you may observe during the Decline step.

» Shows physical and emotional symptoms of stress and becomes accident-prone.

» Dreads going to work.

» Avoids spending additional hours at work during the week or on weekends.

» Relies more on technology to complete tasks and communicate.

» Devotes minimal effort to tasks and projects.

» Withdraws from social interactions with peers and managers.

» Finds legitimate reasons to work remotely.

» Seeks information to validate his position and find fault in others.

» Speaks negatively about the company in social media sites.

» Openly disregards and rejects company logos and symbols.

» Avoids participating in work-related after-hours events.

» Rejects changes.

» Quality of work deteriorates significantly.

Now it's your turn.

Select which behaviors from this list you have noticed among the employees who are in the Decline step in Worksheet 5.5.

Worksheet 5.5 Behaviors Observed From Employees in Decline Step

BEHAVIORS	EMPLOYEE NAMES		
Shows physical and emotional symptoms of stress and becomes accident-prone.			
Dreads going to work.			
Avoids spending additional hours at work during the week or on weekends.			
Relies more on technology to complete tasks and communicate.			
Devotes minimal effort to tasks and projects.			
Withdraws from social interactions with peers and managers.			
Finds legitimate reasons to work remotely.			
Seeks information to validate his position and find fault in others.			
Speaks negatively about the company in social media sites.			
Openly disregards and rejects company logos and symbols.			
Avoids participating in work-related after-hours events.			
Rejects changes.			
Quality of work deteriorates significantly.			

LISTEN UP!

Look for behavior patterns.
Avoid being intrusive.

Manager Dos and Don'ts

Here are some suggestions for you to promote employee engagement during this step—and also tips on what you should not do.

Dos

» Express your concern about the employee's situation.

» Carefully balance positive and developmental feedback.

» Provide pertinent development opportunities.

» Define tasks clearly before assigning them to the employee and communicate quality standards.

» Confirm understanding of instructions.

» Establish realistic and mutually agreed upon timeframes to complete tasks.

» Offer appropriate support for the employee to complete tasks.

» Support and reinforce interactions within the team.

» Maintain the team's routine meetings and activities.

» Reinforce the value of the employee's contributions to the team as applicable.

» Pay close attention to employee signals and behaviors of disengagement.

» Give credit where credit is due.

» Anticipate and remove barriers for employee success.

» Communicate, communicate, and communicate.

» Offer available organizational resources to the employee.

» Acknowledge faults and provide "on-the-spot" corrections.

» Handle performance issues fairly and equitably (workload, work-life balance, performance management).

» Provide dignified options to employees.

» Demonstrate empathy whenever necessary.

» Stay away from gossip.

Don'ts

» Assume.

» Play favorites.

» Foster unrealistic expectations about the employee's opportunities for development in the company.

» Neglect enforcing accountability for quality of work.

» Wait until the last minute to check on the status of tasks.

» Discuss details of private conversations with the employee with other members of the team.

» Reprimand in public.

» Ignore signals and behaviors of engagement or disengagement.

» Be secretive about information that can be shared.

» Provide incorrect information.

» Micromanage.

» Overlook opportunities to recognize and acknowledge employees.

» Be rude, distant, or cold.

» Jump to conclusions.

LISTEN UP!

Define your expectations and confirm that your employees understand. Speak their language.

Now it's your turn.

Worksheet 5.6 presents a behavior self-assessment for you to identify those behaviors that you have displayed or that you display typically. Place a check mark on the right column to indicate if you display those behaviors, you do not display them, or you display them sometimes.

Worksheet 5.6   Manager Behavior Self-Assessment: Decline Step

BEHAVIOR	YES	NO	SOMETIMES
DOS:			
Express your concern about the employee's situation.			
Carefully balance positive and developmental feedback.			
Provide pertinent development opportunities.			
Define tasks clearly before assigning them to the employee and communicate quality standards.			
Confirm understanding of instructions.			
Establish realistic and mutually agreed upon timeframes to complete tasks.			
Offer appropriate support for the employee to complete tasks.			
Support and reinforce interactions within the team.			

BEHAVIOR	YES	NO	SOMETIMES
Maintain the team's routine meetings and activities.			
Reinforce the value of the employee's contributions to the team as applicable.			
Pay close attention to employee signals and behaviors of disengagement.			
Give credit where credit is due.			
Anticipate and remove barriers for employee success.			
Communicate, communicate, and communicate.			
Offer available organizational resources to the employee.			
Acknowledge faults and provide "on-the-spot" corrections.			
Handle performance issues fairly and equitably (workload, work-life balance, performance management).			
Provide dignified options to employees.			
Demonstrate empathy whenever necessary.			
Stay away from gossip.			
DON'TS:			
Assume.			
Play favorites.			
Foster unrealistic expectations about the employee's opportunities for development in the company.			
Neglect enforcing accountability for quality of work.			
Wait until the last minute to check on the status of tasks.			
Discuss details of private conversations with the employee with other members of the team.			
Reprimand in public.			

BEHAVIOR	YES	NO	SOMETIMES
Ignore signals and behaviors of engagement or disengagement.			
Be secretive about information that can be shared.			
Provide incorrect information.			
Micromanage.			
Overlook opportunities to recognize and acknowledge employees.			
Be rude, distant, or cold.			
Jump to conclusions.			

1. How many are dos and how many are don'ts?

_____

_____

_____

2. Identify the three don'ts that you would like to turn into dos.

_____

_____

_____

3. Identify the behaviors that you do sometimes and explain why you do so.

_____

_____

_____

Next, we will wrap up our discussion of the Engagement "I" Path with the final two steps: Stay or Leave and Re-engage or Disengage. At the conclusion of chapter 6 we will summarize what's been presented in part II with a list of key points and takeaways for all the steps.

CHAPTER 6:

Stay or Leave and Re-engage or Disengage

Stay or Leave

Overview

The employee's decision of whether to Stay or Leave the workplace often takes place when an employee reassesses her relationship with the workplace after a period of engagement decline. Like the Critical Incident that we discussed previously, the employee's decision to Stay or Leave is not a step in the Engagement "I" Path, but is rather a turning point that will mark the path the employee will follow. If the employee decides to stay in the company, she will move to the step in the engagement process that we have named Re-engage or Disengage; however, if instead she decides to leave the company physically, mentally, or physically and mentally, the engagement process will end after this turning point.

Please keep in mind that in most cases, employees will not communicate that they are considering leaving the workplace to their managers. Therefore, even if you begin to notice some of the employee behaviors that we present later in this section, your interpretation of their relationship with a possible employee decision to Stay or Leave will be speculative, because the behaviors could be related to something totally extraneous to the workplace. We recommend that you pay special attention to those cues and act only on the basis of facts instead of on rumors or opinions, and that you reach out to the human resources professionals in your company if you have any questions about how to proceed.

Before we continue our discussion, we would like you to continue to identify if any of your employees are in this turning point of the Engagement "I" Path.

Now it's your turn.

Who is in the Stay or Leave turning point? List the names of those employees who are in this stage in Worksheet 6.1.

Worksheet 6.1   Employees in the Stay or Leave Turning Point

	EMPLOYEE NAMES
STAY OR LEAVE	

Drivers

When an employee is making a decision as critical as whether to Stay or Leave the workplace, the following factors will influence his decision: relationships, trust, and total rewards. Let's take a closer look at these drivers within the context of this decision.

The employee's perceptions of present and future availability and distribution of total rewards, such as base pay, incentive pay, and overall benefits, may persuade him to decide to Stay or Leave. The relative importance of these rewards for the employee and his personal circumstances may lead him to decide to stay, particularly if the possibilities of obtaining similar or greater rewards elsewhere are reduced. Let's look at an example.

Hilde has a particular chronic health condition that requires frequent visits to specialists in order for her to live free of pain. Hilde's employer offers a comprehensive health plan that covers her visits with minimal out-of-pocket expenses. Even though Hilde's level of engagement has declined substantially since her assignment to a different unit where she does not feel valued, Hilde will very likely stay at her workplace at least until she finds an opportunity with an employer who will provide similar health coverage.

In contrast, Nancy, Hilde's peer whose level of engagement has also declined, hardly ever visits a medical office. Consequently, Nancy does not have to rely on her employer's comprehensive health plan as much as Hilde. Therefore, Nancy will very likely leave her workplace.

Any changes in those total rewards or in the employee's own personal circumstances may lead the employee to reconsider her decision to stay. For example, if Hilde suddenly finds out that her spouse can include her in a medical plan that offers comparable benefits, she may reconsider or change her initial decision to stay at her workplace.

LISTEN UP!

Employee decisions to Stay or Leave often also depend on factors outside of your control.

We will now share with you some examples of behaviors that you may notice among your employees who are in this turning point of the Engagement "I" Path. At the end of the list, we would like you to identify who is displaying these behaviors as you continue your plans to increase employee engagement.

Employee Behaviors

These are some employee behaviors that you may observe during the time when an employee is making a decision to Stay or Leave.

» Does not seek additional opportunities or responsibilities.

» Finds reasons to justify not participating in projects or activities.

» Responds defensively to feedback.

» Does not show interest in delivering high-quality work.

» Does not detect errors that she would have noticed in the past.

» Avoids sharing meals and breaks from work with peers, managers, and leaders.

- » Maintains brief conversations on very neutral topics.

- » Shows discomfort during long meetings through verbal and nonverbal communication.

- » Only interacts with other team members for task-related purposes.

- » Only displays company logo and other symbols when it is absolutely required.

- » Does not participate in any after-hours work-related activities, without any explanation.

- » Avoids interacting with leaders with whom the employee previously had developed a positive relationship.

- » Is skeptical about the information that he receives about the company.

- » Takes extensive notes during individual meetings with manager.

- » Does not present arguments during performance reviews even if he disagrees with the results.

LISTEN UP!

"Focus on the nonverbal messages."
— Norma Dávila

Now it's your turn.

Select which behaviors from this list you have noticed among the employees who are in the Stay or Leave turning point in Worksheet 6.2.

Worksheet 6.2   Behaviors Observed From Employees in the Stay or Leave Turning Point

BEHAVIORS	EMPLOYEE NAMES		
Does not seek additional opportunities or responsibilities.			
Finds reasons to justify not participating in projects or activities.			
Responds defensively to feedback.			
Does not show interest in delivering high-quality work.			
Does not detect errors that she would have noticed in the past.			
Avoids sharing meals and breaks from work with peers, managers, and leaders.			
Maintains brief conversations on very neutral topics.			
Shows discomfort during long meetings through verbal and nonverbal communication.			
Only interacts with other team members for task-related purposes.			
Only displays company logo and other symbols when it is absolutely required.			
Does not participate in any after-hours work-related activities, without any explanation.			
Avoids interacting with leaders with whom the employee previously had developed a positive relationship.			
Is skeptical about the information that he receives about the company.			
Takes extensive notes during individual meetings with manager.			
Does not present arguments during performance reviews even if he disagrees with the results.			

Manager Dos and Don'ts

Here are some examples of what you should and should not do when an employee is in the Stay or Leave turning point.

Dos

» Provide short-term project assignments and responsibilities.

» Explain the benefits of participating in projects or activities reinforcing the employee's potential contribution.

» Be very aware while providing feedback to avoid emotional triggers for defensiveness.

» Assign tasks that match the competencies of the employee.

» Emphasize the importance of quality in completing tasks without being condescending.

» Ensure that time allotted to complete tasks is realistic.

» Organize activities for the team where all members can share a meal or a break.

» Allow employees flexibility in choosing how to participate in projects.

» Encourage collaboration and support between employees.

» Continue to display company logo and other symbols as customary.

» Emphasize the importance of after-hours work-related activities as part of organizational identity.

» Encourage open discussions about information shared in official forums.

» Demonstrate engagement.

» Clearly define goals, objectives, and expectations.

» Ensure understanding of instructions and deadlines.

» Take notes about key points discussed during individual meetings with the employee.

» Share positive feedback received about the employee as appropriate.

» Show respect and sensitivity when handling delicate performance issues.

Don'ts

» Assume that the employee is ready, willing, and able to complete a project as she has done in the past.

» Expect the employee to be interested in participating in projects and activities that would entail additional work for him.

» Overlook current preferences or other life circumstances that may create discomfort in discussions about projects or activities.

» Disregard the potential emotional impact of feedback on the employee.

» Assign tasks for which the employee does not have the necessary capabilities and competencies.

» Make cynical references to the employee's previous track record when explaining assignments.

» Expect high levels of energy and enthusiasm.

» Force the employee to participate in "gimmicky" team activities in which he feels uncomfortable.

» Overload other team members when an employee's productivity is limited.

» Encourage comments and speculation about the employee's behavior.

» Apply a double-standard for performance among employees.

» Set up goals and objectives that you do not expect the employee to meet.

» Dwell only on negative aspects of performance.

» Raise personal issues of the employee during meetings.

» Comment on your own feelings about the employee and her work or behavior during individual meetings with her or with others.

LISTEN UP!
Beware of fake engagement.

Now it's your turn.

Worksheet 6.3 presents a behavior self-assessment for you to identify those behaviors that you have displayed or that you display typically when an employee is in the Stay or Leave turning point. Place a check mark on the right column to indicate if you display those behaviors, you do not display them, or you display them sometimes.

Worksheet 6.3   Manager Behavior Self-Assessment: Stay or Leave Turning Point

BEHAVIOR	YES	NO	SOMETIMES
DOS:			
Provide short-term project assignments and responsibilities.			
Explain the benefits of participating in projects or activities reinforcing the employee's potential contribution.			
Be very aware while providing feedback to avoid emotional triggers for defensiveness.			
Assign tasks that match the competencies of the employee.			
Emphasize the importance of quality in completing tasks without being condescending.			
Ensure that time allotted to complete tasks is realistic.			

BEHAVIOR	YES	NO	SOMETIMES
Organize activities for the team where all members can share a meal or a break.			
Allow employees flexibility in choosing how to participate in projects.			
Encourage collaboration and support between employees.			
Continue to display company logo and other symbols as customary.			
Emphasize the importance of after-hours work-related activities as part of organizational identity.			
Encourage open discussions about information shared in official forums.			
Demonstrate engagement.			
Clearly define goals, objectives, and expectations.			
Ensure understanding of instructions and deadlines.			
Take notes about key points discussed during individual meetings with the employee.			
Share positive feedback received about the employee as appropriate.			
Show respect and sensitivity when handling delicate performance issues.			
DON'TS:			
Assume that the employee is ready, willing, and able to complete a project as she has done in the past.			
Expect the employee to be interested in participating in projects and activities that would entail additional work for him.			

BEHAVIOR	YES	NO	SOMETIMES
Overlook current preferences or other life circumstances that may create discomfort in discussions about projects or activities.			
Disregard the potential emotional impact of feedback on the employee.			
Assign tasks for which the employee does not have the necessary capabilities and competencies.			
Make cynical references to the employee's previous track record when explaining assignments.			
Expect high levels of energy and enthusiasm.			
Force the employee to participate in "gimmicky" team activities in which he feels uncomfortable.			
Overload other team members when an employee's productivity is limited.			
Encourage comments and speculation about the employee's behavior.			
Apply a double-standard for performance among employees.			
Set up goals and objectives that you do not expect the employee to meet.			
Dwell only on negative aspects of performance.			
Raise personal issues of the employee during meetings.			
Comment on your own feelings about the employee and her work or behavior during individual meetings with her or with others.			

1. How many are dos and how many are don'ts?

   _____

   _____

   _____

2. Identify the three don'ts that you would like to turn into dos.

   _____

   _____

   _____

3. Identify the behaviors that you do sometimes and explain why you do so.

   _____

   _____

   _____

Re-engage or Disengage

Overview

The nature of the relationship with the company, management, and team of an employee who decides to stay at a workplace will be different than it was prior to considering leaving. Typically, an employee who chooses to stay has a less idealistic perception of the workplace than an employee who has never considered the option of working elsewhere. Consequently, his level of engagement will very likely not be as high as that of those other employees.

Upon making the choice to stay in the company, the employee must still make another decision that will affect the path that she will follow in the Engagement "I" Path. The decision of whether to re-engage with or disengage from the company constitutes another one of those turning points in the employee engagement process, just like the decision to Stay or Leave. You may be asking yourself if it is possible for an employee to re-engage.

In Re-engagement, the employee will need to re-establish relationships and reconnect emotionally with the company. However, this employee will be carrying additional emotional loads because, according to the Engagement "I"

Path that we have discussed so far, she has undergone the impact of a Critical Incident, the effects of an engagement decline, and the consequences of a career and personal decision.

An employee who is in Disengagement has not been able to overcome any negative impact of a Critical Incident. As a result, his levels of engagement have continued to decline and, very likely, personal needs and commitments that are beyond your control (as his manager) have fueled the decision to stay in the company. However, since this employee is still a part of your team, you have to be there for him in this step so that he will begin to reconnect with the company; yet, you should acknowledge the fragility of the relationship at this point.

LISTEN UP!
If re-engagement is a possibility, your role as a manager is crucial for your employees to re-engage.

Just like the employee who joins the company and begins moving through the steps of the Engagement "I" Path, reaching the Testing the Waters step after ending the Starting Out step, the employee who chooses to re-engage or to disengage with the workplace will return to the Testing the Waters step to continue her path. Please keep in mind that the employee's relationship with you and with the organization that you represent is very fragile at this step of the Engagement "I" Path and, like a broken glass, it will never go back to what it was before.

LISTEN UP!
Re-engage with your employee as you would like her to re-engage with you. It goes both ways.

Before we continue our discussion, we would like you to continue to identify if any of your employees are in the Re-engage or Disengage turning point of the Engagement "I" Path.

Now it's your turn.

Who is choosing to Re-engage and Disengage in this turning point? List their names in worksheets 6.4 and 6.5.

Worksheet 6.4   Employees in Re-engagement

	EMPLOYEE NAMES
RE-ENGAGEMENT	

Worksheet 6.5   Employees in Disengagement

	EMPLOYEE NAMES
DISENGAGEMENT	

Drivers

The primary engagement drivers that will play a role in an employee's decision to re-engage or disengage are total rewards, performance management, intrinsic motivation, and you.

In this step, external factors play a key role. Total rewards will still be valuable in the decision to re-engage or disengage. For example, an employee may begin to exert a level of effort at work in proportion to the total rewards that he perceives to be receiving; this level of effort may be higher and lead to re-engagement, or lower and lead to disengagement.

Performance management issues related to task distribution, job autonomy, work-life balance, and performance reviews may be important for the employee at this point. He will focus mainly on task completion during regular working hours and meeting objectives to increase the likelihood of still having a position at the company. If the employee perceives a reasonable level of fairness in performance management, and overall, is satisfied with at least how some of those issues are handled, he may begin to re-engage. Otherwise, he will disengage.

An employee who is making these choices may look inward to find a sense of meaning in her work. She tries to find a reason to reconnect emotionally with the workplace or with you as a manager. If the employee cannot discover a new meaning in her work or cannot reconnect emotionally with the workplace or with you as a manager, then her path to re-engagement or disengagement will be entirely contingent on external factors such as those mentioned elsewhere in this book. That emotional connection is what will motivate the employee to work and to put forth the extra effort necessary to succeed in today's business world.

LISTEN UP!

Today's managers need to make sure that employees establish that emotional connection.

Employee Behaviors

These are some employee behaviors that you may observe when an employee is in the Re-engage or Disengage turning point.

> » Seeks opportunities to participate in projects that would increase or decrease her visibility in the company.

> » Adopts a "wait-and-see" attitude about any potential growth opportunities, deciding to take advantage of those that could lead to career development if re-engaging, and passing on them if disengaging.

- » Completes assigned tasks beyond or below expectations.

- » Quantity and quality of work improves or deteriorates.

- » Carefully observes how others react to him and advances toward re-engagement if their reactions are positive, and toward disengagement if their reactions are negative.

- » Self-monitors expressions and behaviors within team interactions, avoiding displays that could lead the team to confirm whether he is re-engaging or disengaging.

- » Questions her own assumptions, beliefs, and values to determine whether to re-engage or disengage.

- » Approaches others, particularly managers, with caution in interactions to avoid revealing information about where he is in the Engagement "I" Path.

- » Controls overtly emotional responses to developmental feedback or any other criticism to avoid demonstrating whether he is re-engaging or disengaging.

LISTEN UP!

Employees will be very careful about they say or do until they make a decision, knowingly or unknowingly.

Now it's your turn.

Select which behaviors from this list you have noticed among the employees who are in the Re-engage or Disengage turning point in Worksheet 6.6.

Worksheet 6.6   Behaviors Observed From Employees in the Re-engage or Disengage Turning Point

BEHAVIORS	EMPLOYEE NAMES		
Seeks or avoids opportunities to participate in projects that would increase or decrease her visibility in the company.			
Adopts a "wait-and-see" attitude about any potential growth opportunities, deciding to take advantage of those that could lead to career development if re-engaging, and passing on them if disengaging.			
Completes assigned tasks beyond or below expectations.			
Quantity and quality of work improves or deteriorates.			
Carefully observes how others react to him, and advances toward re-engagement if their reaction are positive, and toward disengagement if their reaction are negative.			
Self-monitors expressions and behaviors within team interactions, avoiding displays that could lead the team to confirm whether he is re-engaging or disengaging.			
Questions her own assumptions, beliefs, and values to determine whether to re-engage or disengage.			
Approaches others, particularly managers, with caution in interactions to avoid revealing information about where he is in the Engagement "I" Path.			
Controls overtly emotional responses to developmental feedback or any other criticism to avoid demonstrating whether he is re-engaging or disengaging.			

Let's think about those employees who seem to be disengaging.

1.   How many of your employees are disengaged because of a psychological divorce from your company, yet they are still at the workplace?

_____

_____

_____

2. Are those employees productive?

_____

_____

_____

3. Are they poisoning the rest of the group with their negativity?

_____

_____

_____

4. What can you do to mitigate their impact on your team?
    List three actions.

_____

_____

_____

Manager Dos and Don'ts

Here are some examples of what you should and should not do when an employee is in the Re-engage or Disengage turning point.

Dos

» Provide timely and useful positive and developmental feedback.

» Encourage questions and experimentation from employee.

» Create a safe environment to stretch talents and make mistakes.

» Pay close attention to signals and behaviors of re-engagement.

» Encourage the employee to reconnect with peers.

» Provide information as pertinent and available.

» Facilitate interactions with other managers and with members of other teams.

» Ensure the employee's participation in company events of all types.

» Anticipate and remove barriers for the employee's success.

» Specify and clarify roles, responsibilities, and expectations about self, the employee, the team, and others in the company.

» Reward appropriate results and reinforce appropriate behaviors.

» Respect the employee's need for privacy.

» Acknowledge and respect the employee's negative experiences when applicable, but encourage her to move forward.

» Be honest, but carefully.

» Avoid conflicts.

» Avoid "testing the employee."

Don'ts

» Disregard the employee's negative experiences and their possible impact on her.

» Show favoritism in the team.

» Overlook signals and behaviors of re-engagement.

» Provide a very general sketch about business goals without connecting them to how the employee will contribute.

» Demonstrate behaviors that are not consistent with organizational image, values, and principles.

» Assume that the employee will know what he should be doing to become reintegrated in the company.

» Leave expectations about the employee's work undefined.

» Postpone giving positive and developmental feedback to the employee.

» Delay recognizing a job well done.

» Point out cultural mistakes that resulted from not having the appropriate information beforehand.

» Defer answering questions promptly and with not enough information.

- » Criticize the employee in public.
- » Provide inconsistent messages (for example, encourage experimentation, but penalize mistakes).
- » Go back to "old stories."
- » Give too many assignments.

Now it's your turn.

Worksheet 6.7 presents a behavior self-assessment for you to identify those behaviors that you have displayed or that you display typically when an employee is in the Re-engage or Disengage turning point. Place a check mark on the right column to indicate if you display those behaviors, you do not display them, or you display them sometimes.

Worksheet 6.7   Manager Behavior Self-Assessment: Re-engage or Disengage Turning Point

BEHAVIOR	YES	NO	SOMETIMES
DOS:			
Provide timely and useful positive and developmental feedback.			
Encourage questions and experimentation from employee.			
Create a safe environment to stretch talents and make mistakes.			
Pay close attention to signals and behaviors of re-engagement.			
Encourage the employee to reconnect with peers.			
Facilitate interactions with other managers and with members of other teams.			
Ensure the employee's participation in company events of all types.			

BEHAVIOR	YES	NO	SOMETIMES
Anticipate and remove barriers for the employee's success.			
Specify and clarify roles, responsibilities, and expectations about self, employee, team, and others in the company.			
Reward appropriate results and reinforce appropriate behaviors.			
Respect the employee's need for privacy.			
Acknowledge and respect the employee's negative experiences when applicable, but encourage her to move forward.			
Be honest, but carefully.			
Avoid conflicts.			
Avoid "testing the employee."			
DON'TS:			
Disregard the employee's negative experiences and their possible impact on her.			
Show favoritism in the team.			
Overlook signals and behaviors of re-engagement.			
Provide a very general sketch about business goals without connecting them to how the employee will contribute.			
Demonstrate behaviors that are not consistent with organizational image, values, and principles.			
Assume that the employee will know what he should be doing to become reintegrated in the company.			
Leave expectations about the employee's work undefined.			
Postpone giving positive and developmental feedback to the employee.			

BEHAVIOR	YES	NO	SOMETIMES
Delay recognizing a job well done.			
Point out cultural mistakes that resulted from not having the appropriate information beforehand.			
Defer answering questions promptly and with not enough information.			
Criticize the employee in public.			
Provide inconsistent messages (for example, encourage experimentation, but penalize mistakes).			
Go back to "old stories."			
Give too many assignments.			

1. How many are dos and how many are don'ts?

    _____

    _____

    _____

2. Identify the three don'ts that you would like to turn into dos.

    _____

    _____

    _____

3. Identify the behaviors that you do sometimes and explain why
    you do so.

    _____

    _____

    _____

KEY POINTS AND TAKEAWAYS FROM PART II

- Engagement is a process.
- Employee engagement levels adjust according to an employee's career and personal circumstances.
- Revisit the model: Engagement "I" Path, Figure 1.
- Be aware of the process: Starting Out, Testing the Waters, Stable, Critical Incident, Growth, Decline, Stay or Leave, Re-engage or Disengage.
- Organizational branding and image "draw" the organizational picture for the employee.
- Respect commitments for total rewards.
- Take into consideration intrinsic motivation.
- Employees are testing you as well.
- Verify your dos and don'ts.
- Critical Incidents are turning points.
- Anticipate the questions. Anticipate the needs.
- Perceptions of fairness and transparency will modify the engagement level.
- Re-engagement cannot be imposed.
- Communication is a key component throughout the entire Engagement "I" Path.

PART III

Employee Engagement Throughout the Employee's Career: Career "I" Path

Introduction

We already discussed the Engagement "I" Path and its steps. Based on our research and our work, we have concluded that employees go through different steps in engagement in a company as they move through stages of their careers. In part III, chapters 7 and 8, we discuss employee engagement through an employee's career. We also show how we see the process of employee engagement and its steps as related to the stages of engagement through an employee's career. As you read these chapters, we encourage you to keep in mind that today's workforce is composed of many individuals who have had or will have multiple jobs and experiences.

In part III, we delve into what happens at each stage of the employee's career and return to the drivers of engagement to emphasize which ones are more important at each stage. We also indicate some of the behaviors that employees tend to display in each one of those stages. At the end of our discussion of each stage, we suggest what you, as a manager, should and should not do to promote employee engagement at each one.

We will guide you again to think about the information that we have shared with you through questions at the end of each section. We hope that by answering these questions, you will be able to apply what you have learned to your particular circumstances.

We will now introduce our view of the stages of engagement in an employee's career and then discuss each one of those stages in further detail.

Stages of Engagement in an Employee's Career: Career "I" Path

When an employee begins her career, either because it is her first job or because she has recently changed careers, she is at the Just Beginning stage. Afterward, she moves to the Getting Settled stage, where she masters the requirements of the position and feels comfortable with what she is doing, perhaps consequently moving into what is commonly known as a comfort zone. When an employee reaches a point where she believes that she has mastered the responsibilities of the position and needs to do something else to continue growing, she begins the Looking for More stage. Once she obtains a new role or position and begins to meet those needs with a sustainable level of mastery, she decides to focus on maintaining such level of performance in the Riding the Tide stage. Afterward, she develops a sense of having completed everything that she thought was possible in the career and reaches the Mission Accomplished stage. During this stage, she begins to ponder about what to do next either in this particular career or as a professional; some employees stay in the Mission Accomplished stage during an extended period of time while others go quickly to the Moving On stage. When it is time to start another career, the employee enters the Moving On stage and returns to Just Beginning. In contrast, the career of an employee who chooses to leave the workforce altogether after the Moving On stage will end. Figure 2 presents a graphic representation of how we view these stages of the Career "I" Path.

We will now discuss each one of these stages. Chapter 7 covers Just Beginning, Getting Settled, and Looking for More. In chapter 8 we'll wrap up the path with Riding the Tide, Mission Accomplished, and Moving On.

Figure 2   Career "I" Path

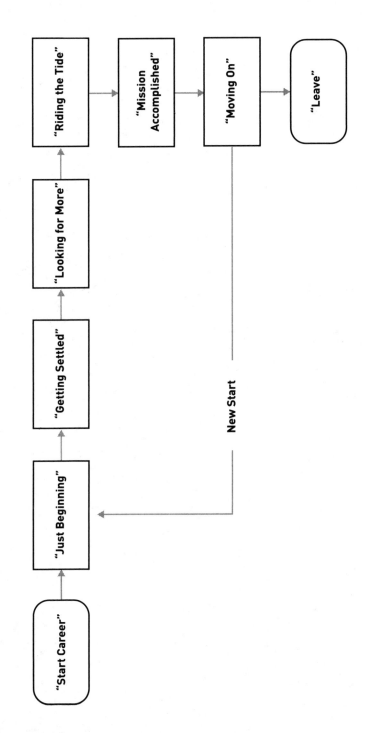

CHAPTER 7:

Just Beginning, Getting Settled, and Looking for More

Just Beginning

Overview

This stage represents the first step in a chosen or discovered field. What happens in this stage is significant; as a result of their experiences, employees will be making decisions about whether this field or position will become a long-term career or a step in their search for the right career for them. Every experience is a new one, so your role as a manager is to make sure that those experiences are remarkable.

In this stage, the employee may be perceived as "the new kid on the block," who is full of ideas and lacks experience—whether this is his first position as a working professional or just the first position in a new career, level, or company. Consequently, others who resist new ideas may disregard his proposals for many reasons, including: "we tried that before and it did not work," "upper management will not buy that," or "let me show you how we do things around here." In contrast, those who are open to new possibilities may welcome the new, refreshing point of view of someone; some of them may even offer to open doors and mentor this employee. Your role as a manager is to support the employee in this transition, reinforcing the value of new ideas and contributions.

LISTEN UP!

The question is the answer.

As "the new kid on the block," this employee may feel the need to prove his worth more than someone who already has a reputation in a particular field. This need may be either self-imposed or a result of expectations established during the recruitment process. Either way, your role as a manager is to allow the employee to demonstrate success without restricting opportunities to learn, and to support him in the journey up the learning curve. You may also be able to modify those expectations if you think that they are unreasonable or unattainable under current circumstances, which shows you support your employee's success. At the same time, you may need to address any concerns of team members related to positive or negative reactions to the newcomer.

This employee probably has different views of herself and the organization, perhaps because of lack of experience. For example, the employee may overrate or underrate her own competencies, thus failing to appropriately match her capabilities with the tasks assigned. As a consequence, she may obtain less than optimal results either because she needs additional time, information, training, and resources or because she is not demonstrating her own true potential. This employee may also have an idealized, stereotypical, positive, or negative view of the company based only on its public image or particular events because she lacks valid criteria against which to compare the company. Before we continue our discussion of the Just Beginning stage, we would like you to identify in which stage of their careers your employees are.

LISTEN UP!

Make your employees feel welcome and valued.

Now it's your turn.

Who is in the Just Beginning stage? List the names of those employees who are in this stage in Worksheet 7.1.

Worksheet 7.1   Employees in the Just Beginning Stage

	EMPLOYEE NAMES
JUST BEGINNING	

Drivers

An employee who is in the Just Beginning stage derives a strong sense of satisfaction from his work. He is excited about the future and eager to determine to what his choices led, partially based on career image. An employee who sees his current role as just a job is less likely to be highly engaged than one who defines the same role as a step in a career. On the contrary, an employee who sees the current role as a step in a career or as part of something else that will transcend any particular organization's boundaries will probably be more engaged.

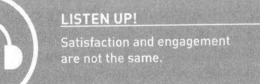

LISTEN UP!
Satisfaction and engagement are not the same.

Intrinsic motivation, defined elsewhere in this book, is a strong driver of engagement at this stage as the employee finds an inner power to focus energy onto the tasks at hand. You as a manager have a priceless opportunity to positively influence the experience of this employee as you capitalize on that intrinsic motivation through balance in total rewards and performance management.

Total rewards are an important component of the Just Beginning stage because the employee's acceptance of the offer to join the organization may be greatly influenced by their composition. The combination of base pay, incentive pay, and overall benefits, as well as organizational image and perceived reputation, is often the decisive factor to accept an offer, along with potential development opportunities in the company. Employees will try to assess what possibilities are available to grow, even if not thinking about the immediate future. You as a manager should be aware of this need and ensure that those rewards, particularly those related to growth and development, are available or potentially available for the employee—while always addressing any concerns or unrealistic expectations.

LISTEN UP!

Keep expectations grounded in reality.

Because this employee will compare subsequent experiences with those that he had in previous positions, you as a manager need to maintain fairness and objectivity, reinforce and reward appropriate behaviors, and become a positive role model to maximize every chance to foster employee engagement with the organization and with you as the manager.

Employee Behaviors

These are some behaviors that you may observe when an employee is in the Just Beginning stage.

> » Expresses a need to speak positively about the organization
>   and show pride in belonging to it.

» Eagerly seeks opportunities to grow and learn inside as well as outside of the organization.

» Creates an image based on the chosen field's models in terms of appearance, vocabulary, and activities, among other components.

» May try to convey more experience in the field than what is real.

» Compares herself with peers in terms of image, accomplishments, projects, and income.

» Experiments with different work habits and routines.

» Networks to make friends and meet mentors.

» Seeks information about expectations in general.

Now it's your turn.

Select which behaviors from this list you have observed among the employees who are in the Just Beginning stage in Worksheet 7.2.

Worksheet 7.2   Behaviors Observed From Employees in Just Beginning Stage

BEHAVIORS	EMPLOYEE NAMES		
Expresses a need to speak positively about the organization and show pride in belonging to it.			
Eagerly seeks opportunities to grow and learn inside as well as outside of the organization.			
Creates an image based on the chosen field's models in terms of appearance, vocabulary, and activities, among other components.			
May try to convey more experience in the field than what is real.			
Compares herself with peers in terms of image, accomplishments, projects, and income.			
Experiments with different work habits and routines.			
Networks to make friends and meet mentors.			
Seeks information about expectations in general.			

Manager Dos and Don'ts

Here are some examples of what you should and should not do when an employee is in the Just Beginning stage.

Dos

> » Allow them to voice their ideas.
>
> » Give opportunities to explore what the employee can do and stretch his abilities.
>
> » Allow experimentation.
>
> » Foster connection between you as a manager and the employee.
>
> » Explain goals and objectives as well as all aspects of performance management.
>
> » Reward and reinforce.
>
> » Provide resources to do the job.
>
> » Show "the company's way of doing things."
>
> » Show appropriate behaviors for the organization and the position.

Don'ts

> » Provide incomplete information.
>
> » Limit the employee's involvement in the organization "because it is too early for you to do X or Y."
>
> » Discourage participation.
>
> » Micromanage the employee.
>
> » Penalize for mistakes.
>
> » Deny opportunities to the employee for which he is qualified (hoarding talent or killing it).
>
> » Leave employee to her own means to find what she needs.
>
> » Discriminate against the employee because she is new to the position, career, or profession and "has much to learn."
>
> » Assume that he knows the "rules."

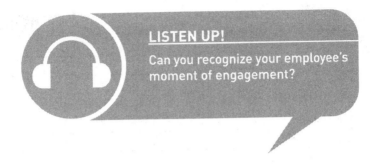

LISTEN UP!

Can you recognize your employee's moment of engagement?

Now it's your turn.

Worksheet 7.3 presents a behavior self-assessment for you to identify those behaviors that you have displayed or that you display typically. Place a check mark on the right column to indicate if you display those behaviors, you do not display them, or you display them sometimes.

Worksheet 7.3   Manager Behavior Self-Assessment: Just Beginning Stage

BEHAVIOR	YES	NO	SOMETIMES
DOS:			
Allow them to voice their ideas.			
Give opportunities to explore what the employee can do and stretch his abilities.			
Allow experimentation.			
Foster connection between you as a manager and the employee.			
Explain goals and objectives as well as all aspects of performance management.			
Reward and reinforce.			
Provide resources to do the job.			
Show "the company's way of doing things."			
Show appropriate behaviors for the organization and the position.			

BEHAVIOR	YES	NO	SOMETIMES
DON'TS:			
Provide incomplete information.			
Limit the employee's involvement in the organization "because it is too early for you to do X or Y."			
Discourage participation.			
Micromanage the employee.			
Penalize for mistakes.			
Deny opportunities to the employee for which he is qualified (hoarding talent or killing it).			
Leave employee to her own means to find what she needs.			
Discriminate against the employee because she is new to the position, career, or profession and "has much to learn."			
Assume that he knows the "rules."			

1. How many are dos and how many are don'ts?

_____

_____

_____

_____

2. Identify the three don'ts that you would like to turn into dos.

_____

_____

_____

_____

3. Identify the behaviors that you do sometimes and explain why you do so.

_____

_____

_____

_____

Getting Settled
Overview

Steadiness and stability are the most significant descriptors of this stage. The employee has gained some experience in the field and career so he exudes more confidence. His focus changes to getting and maintaining a reputation in the field in the company as well as outside of it as he defines a professional niche. As a consequence, he makes every possible effort to stay up to date in the chosen field and to consistently demonstrate that knowledge to become known as an expert or "go to" person. Before we continue our discussion of the Getting Settled stage, we would like you to identify in which stage of their careers your employees are.

Now it's your turn.

Who is in the Getting Settled stage? List the names of those employees who are in this stage in Worksheet 7.4.

Worksheet 7.4   *Employees in the Getting Settled Stage*

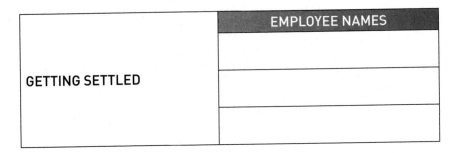

	EMPLOYEE NAMES
GETTING SETTLED	

Drivers

In the Getting Settled stage, the employee has already defined what the current position is and has generally accepted that definition as her reality. Therefore, the importance of the employee's lens about her autonomy as a driver of employee engagement diminishes unless an unforeseen event takes place. The nature of the possible event and how it is handled may have an effect on that lens, which may be similar to when a Critical Incident alters the course of the employee's path through the Engagement "I" Path.

At this stage, the employee will focus on benefits, image, and environment that were offered prior to joining the company because she will have more time to find out if they will be available and the conditions under which they will be available. It is important for you as a manager to provide recognitions, incentives, and opportunities, so we recommend that you keep in mind that the employee will be most attentive for information and availability about those rewards.

Communication will be a driver of employee engagement at this stage. Formal communication are the mechanism through which the employee receives official information about the organization and compares it to her on-the-job experiences as well as to what she gets through unofficial channels such as the office grapevine.

Performance management continues to be a driver of employee engagement at this stage. As the employee seeks stability, he also strengthens the relationship with you as a manager. How you conduct different aspects of performance management, such as rewards and recognition as well as career opportunities, may be a factor in whether the employee is engaged with you regardless of other aspects of his experience with the organization or even with the chosen field in general. You as a manager are the architect of that relationship.

LISTEN UP!

Are you ready to pursue your employee's engagement?

Employee Behaviors

These are some behaviors that you may observe when an employee is in the Getting Settled stage.

» Networks to become known in the field as an expert because the purpose of networking changes as he seeks stability in the chosen field and career.

» Gets involved in professional organizations to build a reputation as an expert.

» Becomes more goal-oriented and strategic in the use of time and energy.

» May display signs of being engaged with the organization, the manager, or both.

» Follows a defined work style as well as work habits and routines.

» Demonstrates that he has a more realistic view of the career or field in the way that he speaks about it.

Now it's your turn.

Select which behaviors from this list you have observed among the employees who are in the Getting Settled stage in Worksheet 7.5.

Worksheet 7.5.   Behaviors Observed From Employees in Getting Settled Stage

BEHAVIORS	EMPLOYEE NAMES		
Networks to become known in the field as an expert because the purpose of networking changes as he seeks stability in the chosen field and career.			
Gets involved in professional organizations to build a reputation as an expert.			
Becomes more goal-oriented and strategic in the use of time and energy.			
May display signs of being engaged with the organization, the manager, or both.			

Follows a defined work style as well as work habits and routines.			
Demonstrates that he has a more realistic view of the career or field in the way that he speaks about it.			

Manager Dos and Don'ts

Here are some examples of what you should and should not do when an employee is in the Getting Settled stage.

Dos

- » Model appropriate behaviors.

- » Communicate, communicate, and communicate.

- » Reward and reinforce.

- » Provide resources to do the job.

- » Be fair in all aspects of performance management, providing flexibility whenever appropriate.

- » Deliver on promises.

- » Maintain a good relationship with the employee as a way to find out what she needs and what she wants for the future.

- » Offer opportunities to grow and develop even if these are lateral moves.

Don'ts

- » Withhold information from the employee.

- » Postpone opportunities to reward and reinforce.

- » Withhold resources to do the job.

- » Discriminate against the employee in performance management "because she is in a comfort zone and does not want to move."

- » Withhold rewards and benefits because of above.

- » Offer growth and development opportunities to other employees because of arbitrary reasons.

» Become detached from the employee because she is not the "flavor of the month."

» Use only electronic means to communicate.

Now it's your turn.

Worksheet 7.6 presents a behavior self-assessment for you to identify those behaviors that you have displayed or that you display typically. Place a check mark on the right column to indicate if you display those behaviors, you do not display them, or you display them sometimes.

Worksheet 7.6   **Manager Behavior Self-Assessment: Getting Settled Stage**

BEHAVIOR	YES	NO	SOMETIMES
DOS:			
Model appropriate behaviors.			
Communicate, communicate, and communicate.			
Reward and reinforce.			
Provide resources to do the job.			
Be fair in all aspects of performance management, providing flexibility whenever appropriate.			
Deliver on promises.			
Maintain a good relationship with the employee as a way to find out what she needs and what she wants for the future.			
Offer opportunities to grow and develop even if these are lateral moves.			
DON'TS			
Withhold information from the employee.			
Postpone opportunities to reward and reinforce.			
Withhold resources to do the job.			

BEHAVIOR	YES	NO	SOMETIMES
Discriminate against the employee in performance management "because she is in a comfort zone and does not want to move."			
Withhold rewards and benefits because of above.			
Offer growth and development opportunities to other employees because of arbitrary reasons.			
Become detached from the employee because she is not the "flavor of the month."			
Use only electronic means to communicate.			

1. How many are dos and how many are don'ts?

_____

_____

_____

2. Identify the three don'ts that you would like to turn into dos.

_____

_____

_____

3. Identify the behaviors that you do sometimes and explain why you do so.

_____

_____

_____

Looking for More

Overview

In this stage, the employee has already significant experience in the field. Usually, after careful thought and consideration or insistence from friends and family members, he begins to realize that he has already accomplished what he could in the current role. Consequently, he begins to inquire about what else he could do—either in his current role through projects or other assignments, or elsewhere in the company where his experiences could be valuable. At this point, the employee is not usually inclined to leave the organization because he is still engaged with it. Therefore, you as a manager have another distinctive opportunity to sway his engagement positively depending on how you address those needs. Before we continue our discussion of the Looking for More stage, we would like you to identify in which stage of their careers your employees are.

Now it's your turn.

Who is in the Looking for More stage? List the names of those employees who are in this stage in Worksheet 7.7.

Worksheet 7.7   *Employees in the Looking for More Stage*

	EMPLOYEE NAMES
LOOKING FOR MORE	

Drivers

As suggested in our overview of this stage, career opportunities within the company will be a major driver of employee engagement because by now the employee has created some expectations about the future. You as a manager will need to address the availability of those opportunities, and your employee's expectations of them, such as stretch assignments, lateral moves, or vertical moves. We invite you to be particularly thoughtful when you plan for discussions about career opportunities with your employee, particularly if you disagree with her self-assessment of her qualifications, because any misunderstandings may lead to hurt feelings that in the end could result in lower engagement with the organization or with you.

LISTEN UP!

Career opportunities come in a variety of forms.

Incentive pay drives engagement at this stage because the employee may decide to stay at the current role in the company instead of actively seeking something else to do if she receives incentive pay for particular accomplishments. You as a manager shall keep in mind that this employee masters the role.

Offering flexibility in working arrangements and schedules may be something to consider while exploring options for this employee who may re-examine his decision to stay in the company if he does not receive something in return for long-term performance and loyalty.

Employee Behaviors

These are some behaviors that you may observe when an employee is in the Looking for More stage.

» Networks to find out about growth opportunities in the organization and outside of it.

» Compares himself with peers looking for a competitive advantage for those opportunities.

» Seeks visibility from other levels of management at every opportunity.

» Shows signs of being engaged with the organization, but not necessarily with the manager.

» Looks for learning opportunities to build marketable skills inside and outside of the organization.

» Makes efforts to market herself for other potential roles.

Now it's your turn.

Select which behaviors from this list you have observed among the employees who are in the Looking for More stage in Worksheet 7.8.

Worksheet 7.8   Behaviors Observed From Employees in Looking for More Stage

BEHAVIORS	EMPLOYEE NAMES		
Networks to find out about growth opportunities in the organization and outside of it.			
Compares himself with peers looking for a competitive advantage for those opportunities.			
Seeks visibility from other levels of management at every opportunity.			
Shows signs of being engaged with the organization, but not necessarily with the manager.			
Looks for learning opportunities to build marketable skills inside and outside of the organization.			
Makes efforts to market herself for other potential roles.			

Manager Dos and Don'ts

Here are some examples of what you should and should not do when an employee is in the Looking for More stage.

Dos

» Provide relevant tasks.

» Find opportunities and projects for development.

» Be fair in all aspects of performance management.

» Offer flexibility and options to work differently.

» Continue a balanced relationship with the employee.

» Communicate information about the future as pertinent to maintain hope and focus on what is next.

» Provide positive feedback.

Don'ts

- » Deny opportunities and projects for development based on an assumption that the employee is getting ready to leave.

- » Discriminate against the employee in performance management issues based on an assumption that the employee is getting ready to leave.

- » Disregard the importance of employee comments.

- » Withhold incentive pay and rewards.

- » Become detached from the employee or rely only on electronic means to communicate.

- » Withhold information about the future.

Now it's your turn.

Worksheet 7.9 presents a behavior self-assessment for you to identify those behaviors that you have displayed or that you display typically. Place a check mark on the right column to indicate if you display those behaviors, you do not display them, or you display them sometimes.

Worksheet 7.9   Manager Behavior Self-Assessment: Looking for More Stage

BEHAVIOR	YES	NO	SOMETIMES
DOS:			
Provide relevant tasks.			
Find opportunities and projects for development.			
Be fair in all aspects of performance management.			
Offer flexibility and options to work differently.			
Continue a balanced relationship with the employee.			

BEHAVIOR	YES	NO	SOMETIMES
Communicate information about the future as pertinent to maintain hope and focus on what is next.			
Provide positive feedback.			
DON'TS:			
Deny opportunities and projects for development based on an assumption that the employee is getting ready to leave.			
Discriminate against the employee in performance management issues based on an assumption that the employee is getting ready to leave.			
Disregard the importance of employee comments.			
Withhold incentive pay and rewards.			
Become detached from the employee or rely only on electronic means to communicate.			
Withhold information about the future.			

1. How many are dos and how many are don'ts?

   _____

   _____

   _____

   _____

2. Identify the three don'ts that you would like to turn into dos.

   _____

   _____

   _____

   _____

3. Identify the behaviors that you do sometimes and explain why you do so.

_____

_____

_____

_____

In the next chapter we'll explore the next stages: Riding the Tide, Mission Accomplished, and Moving On.

LISTEN UP!

Simply put: Don't withhold.

CHAPTER 8:

Riding the Tide, Mission Accomplished, and Moving On

Riding the Tide
Overview

This stage entails a return to stability and consistency after obtaining a promotion or opportunity and making a decision to stay in the chosen field for a long time. The employee who reaches this stage has amassed a wealth of experience that allows him to considerably reduce the learning curve in any new project or assignment. Thus, he quickly gains and projects confidence in any new role. At this stage, the employee will again focus on getting and maintaining a reputation in the company as well as outside of it. Even though he seeks stability and consistency in the new role, the employee who reaches this stage will challenge himself to stay up to date in the field as a mechanism to ward off obsolescence.

As a manager, you face the challenge of maintaining this employee's engagement with you and the company as you support him in defining any new roles and in obtaining stability and consistency again. Before we continue our discussion of the Riding the Tide stage, we would like you to identify in which stage of their careers your employees are.

Now it's your turn.

Who is in the Riding the Tide stage? List the names of those employees who are in this stage in Worksheet 8.1.

Worksheet 8.1   Employees in Riding the Tide Stage

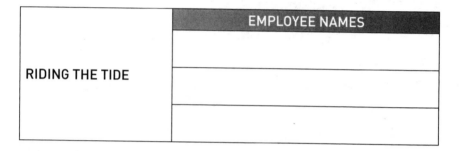

	EMPLOYEE NAMES
RIDING THE TIDE	

Drivers

An employee who reaches this stage has already accepted reality. Unless an unforeseen event takes place in this stage that transforms this point of view, the lens shall remain the same. We encourage you to remain vigilant for any potential signs of changes in this lens because they may lead to a dramatic shift in employee engagement at this stage. For instance, an employee who suddenly decides he views his current role as a job instead of a career will very likely become less engaged than one who suddenly decides the opposite. Consequently, you will need to adjust how you work with those employees to foster their engagement.

Total rewards will continue to be a driver of engagement at this stage because the employee will focus once more on what is available for her and perhaps even more so, because she craves stability and consistency for the rest of her career, which could be the rest of her tenure in the company. Therefore, any negative deviations between what was offered and what is actually delivered may lead to highly emotional reactions and disagreements that eventually may lead to lower levels of engagement. Conversely, any positive deviations may eventually lead to higher levels of engagement.

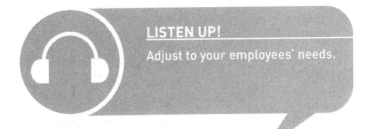

LISTEN UP!

Adjust to your employees' needs.

Performance management is very important as a driver of employee engagement at this stage. However, because of this stage's focus on stability, as a manager, you need to become even more acutely aware of how your employee may perceive the different aspects of this driver that we have discussed so far. We suggest that you pay particular attention to how you allocate recognition since this is a particularly sensitive issue for employees who have advanced this far in their careers. We also emphasize the importance of those seemingly small gestures, such as flexibility and recognition, as well as a simple "thank you," which may become more salient at a stage where the employee may believe that he has earned certain rights. Once more, the source, nature, and frequency of communication may guide an employee toward lower or higher levels of engagement, particularly for an employee who is at a stage where workplace fluctuations are less welcome than perhaps in previous stages.

LISTEN UP!

Employees don't want to fail.

Employee Behaviors

These are some behaviors that you may observe when an employee is in the Riding the Tide stage.

> » Shows signs of being engaged with the organization even though the level of engagement may vary.

» Demonstrates or verbalizes that he sees the manager as someone who will eventually move on because he perceives managers as having more mobility tied to opportunities than employees in the company.

» Complies with requests and may seem to enjoy work.

» Stays active in different networks as a means to obtain and share information as well as maintain his reputation.

» Maintains steady, perhaps optimal, level of performance without any major variations.

» Embraces high standards.

» Analyzes the value of additional challenges or assignments that would entail additional expenditures of energy.

» Periodically analyzes the costs and benefits of making additional moves, typically deciding to stay in the current state.

» Expresses higher expectations.

Now it's your turn.

Select which behaviors from this list you have observed among the employees who are in the Riding the Tide stage in Worksheet 8.2.

Worksheet 8.2   Behaviors Observed From Employees in Riding the Tide Stage

BEHAVIORS	EMPLOYEE NAMES
Shows signs of being engaged with the organization even though the level of engagement may vary.	
Demonstrates or verbalizes that he sees the manager as someone who will eventually move on because he perceives managers as having more mobility tied to opportunities than employees in the company.	
Complies with requests and may seem to enjoy work.	

BEHAVIORS	EMPLOYEE NAMES
Stays active in different networks as a means to obtain and share information as well as maintain his reputation.	
Maintains steady, perhaps optimal, level of performance without any major variations.	
Embraces high standards.	
Analyzes the value of additional challenges or assignments that would entail additional expenditures of energy.	
Periodically analyzes the costs and benefits of making additional moves, typically deciding to stay in the current state.	
Expresses higher expectations.	

Manager Dos and Don'ts

Here are some examples of what you should and should not do when an employee is in the Riding the Tide stage.

Dos

- » Be clear about goals and expectations.
- » Continue to find opportunities and projects for development.
- » Communicate information about the future as pertinent to maintain hope and focus on what is next.
- » Assume that total rewards were delivered as offered.
- » Listen to "the words behind the words."
- » Communicate, communicate, and communicate about the present and future.
- » Maintain a balanced relationship with the employee and continue to seek information about what she needs.
- » Allow the employee to go beyond the job's requirements.
- » Meet often with the employee.
- » Maintain the focus.

» Reward and reinforce as appropriate.

» Be respectful of the employee.

Don'ts

» Withhold total rewards "because she will be here forever."

» Limit flexibility in work arrangements and other aspects of performance management because those resources should be spent on employees who are joining the organization and can contribute more.

» Withhold information from the employee.

» Become detached from the employee and rely only on electronic means to communicate because "she knows the rules."

» Postpone decisions or opportunities to reward and recognize the employee.

LISTEN UP!

Maintain your focus.

Now it's your turn.

Worksheet 8.3 presents a behavior self-assessment for you to identify those behaviors that you have displayed or that you display typically. Place a check mark on the right column to indicate if you display those behaviors, you do not display them, or you display them sometimes.

Worksheet 8.3   **Manager Behavior Self-Assessment:**
Riding the Tide Stage

BEHAVIOR	YES	NO	SOMETIMES
DOS:			
Be clear about goals and expectations.			
Continue to find opportunities and projects for development.			
Communicate information about the future as pertinent to maintain hope and focus on what is next.			
Assume that total rewards were delivered as offered.			
Listen to "the words behind the words."			
Communicate, communicate, and communicate about the present and future.			
Maintain a balanced relationship with the employee and continue to seek information about what she needs.			
Allow the employee to go beyond the job's requirements.			
Meet often with the employee.			
Maintain the focus.			
Reward and reinforce as appropriate.			
Be respectful of the employee.			
DON'TS:			
Withhold total rewards "because she will be here forever."			
Limit flexibility in work arrangements and other aspects of performance management because those resources should be spent on employees who are joining the organization and can contribute more.			
Withhold information from the employee.			

BEHAVIOR	YES	NO	SOMETIMES
Become detached from the employee and rely only on electronic means to communicate because "she knows the rules."			
Postpone decisions or opportunities to reward and recognize the employee.			

1. How many are dos and how many are don'ts?

2. Identify the three don'ts that you would like to turn into dos.

3. Identify the behaviors that you do sometimes and explain why you do so.

Mission Accomplished

Overview

An employee who reaches this stage is already established in the field. At this point, she has realized that she has already obtained maximum benefit and growth from the particular workplace or from the chosen career. Typically, an employee who reaches this stage is either extremely satisfied or extremely unsatisfied with her progress to date. Therefore, she faces three choices for her future: to go to another workplace, to start a new career, or to leave the workforce altogether.

This employee may still feel some emotional connection to the workplace or, in rare instances, with the manager. However, she has already started the process to emotionally detach from the company in an effort to diminish the emotional impact of the upcoming separation.

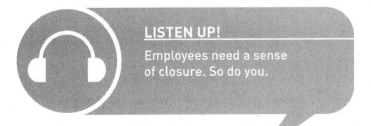

LISTEN UP!
Employees need a sense of closure. So do you.

Before we proceed to our discussion of the drivers of the Mission Accomplished stage, we would like you to identify in which stage of their careers your employees are.

Now it's your turn.

Who is in the Mission Accomplished stage? List the names of those employees who are in this stage in Worksheet 8.4.

Worksheet 8.4 Employees in Mission Accomplished Stage

	EMPLOYEE NAMES
MISSION ACCOMPLISHED	

Drivers

At the Mission Accomplished stage, the employee will be acting on the assumption that he will move on to do something else or to do it somewhere else.

Therefore, he will focus on closing unfinished business and having a positive experience through his remaining time at the company until he is ready for the next stage.

Organizational brand and image will be important because the employee will remember the virtues more than the shortcomings of the company where he spent part of his career. However, performance management will be the most important driver of employee engagement at this stage because the employee will be particularly observant of how he is treated at the end of his career or tenure at the company. Issues related to rewards and recognition will be prominent because the employee expects some type of acknowledgment for what he has done in his field at the company. Similarly, other employees who may be approaching the Mission Accomplished stage may envision how their own performance may be managed in that stage in the future.

Although the duration of the Mission Accomplished stage may vary between employees, those who are in it will influence other employees and their level of engagement. Thus, as a manager, you should continue to work with an employee who is in the Mission Accomplished stage just like you do with those employees who are in other stages. Please keep in mind that, even if this employee is already disengaged, he may try to display the opposite for the sake of appearances until it is time to leave the company.

LISTEN UP!

Are you a role model of how to treat employees? It's all about engagement!

Employee Behaviors

The following is a list of some employee behaviors that you may observe during the Mission Accomplished stage.

> » Shows subtle and not so subtle signs of disengagement with the organization and manager, such as nonverbal signs of disinterest in the chosen field.

» Pays special attention in conversations about development opportunities in other organizations and about who has left the organization to do something else.

» Reactivates latent networks to find opportunities to pursue other interests.

» Shifts conversations to remembering past successes and accomplishments whenever possible.

» Dedicates the requested amount of effort to tasks.

» Previous level of performance changes to better or worse.

Now it's your turn.

Select which behaviors from this list you have observed among the employees who are in the Mission Accomplished stage in Worksheet 8.5.

Worksheet 8.5 *Behaviors Observed From Employees in Mission Accomplished Stage*

BEHAVIORS	EMPLOYEE NAMES		
Shows subtle and not so subtle signs of disengagement with the organization and manager, such as nonverbal signs of disinterest in the chosen field.			
Pays special attention in conversations about development opportunities in other organizations and about who has left the organization to do something else.			
Reactivates latent networks to find opportunities to pursue other interests.			
Shifts conversations to remembering past successes and accomplishments whenever possible.			
Dedicates the requested amount of effort to tasks.			
Previous level of performance changes to better or worse.			

Manager Dos and Don'ts

Here are some examples of what you should and should not do when an employee is in the Mission Accomplished stage.

Dos

- » Respect the employee.
- » Manage your emotions, whether they are good or bad.
- » Value the employee's contributions privately and publicly.
- » Reward and recognize as appropriate.
- » Focus on positives as much as possible.
- » Maintain the relationship with the employee as positive as possible.
- » Communicate, communicate, and communicate as usual.
- » Value and show deference for contributions.
- » Give time and be there.
- » Tackle issues "straight and to the point."

Don'ts

- » Convey mixed messages.
- » Deny opportunities and projects for development based on an assumption that the employee is approaching the end of his tenure in the organization.
- » Discriminate against an employee in performance management the issues based on the assumption that the employee is getting ready to leave or is not paying attention.
- » Focus on the negative aspects of the workplace as well as of his performance.
- » Fail to listen.
- » Minimize value of contributions.
- » Withhold incentive pay and rewards.
- » Lack empathy.

» Dedicate less time to the employee because he seems like he is about to leave.

» Try to interfere with the employee's decisions in this stage.

» Provide less information because he may be going elsewhere and may take that information.

» Postpone or cancel recognitions, rewards, or bonuses.

Now it's your turn.

Worksheet 8.6 presents a behavior self-assessment for you to identify those behaviors that you have displayed or that you display typically. Place a check mark on the right column to indicate if you display those behaviors, you do not display them, or you display them sometimes.

Worksheet 8.6 **Manager Behavior Self-Assessment: Mission Accomplished Stage**

BEHAVIOR	YES	NO	SOMETIMES
DOS:			
Respect the employee.			
Manage your emotions, whether they are good or bad.			
Value the employee's contributions privately and publicly.			
Reward and recognize as appropriate.			
Focus on positives as much as possible.			
Maintain the relationship with the employee as positive as possible.			
Communicate, communicate, and communicate as usual.			
Value and show deference for contributions.			
Give time and be there.			

Chapter 8

BEHAVIOR	YES	NO	SOMETIMES
Tackle issues "straight and to the point."			
DON'TS:			
Convey mixed messages.			
Deny opportunities and projects for development based on an assumption that the employee is approaching the end of his tenure in the organization.			
Discriminate against the employee in performance management issues based on an assumption that the employee is getting ready to leave or is not paying attention.			
Focus on the negative aspects of the workplace as well as of his performance.			
Fail to listen.			
Minimize value of contributions.			
Withhold incentive pay and rewards.			
Lack empathy.			
Dedicate less time to the employee because he seems like he is about to leave.			
Try to interfere with the employee's decisions in this stage.			
Provide less information because he may be going elsewhere and may take that information.			
Postpone or cancel recognitions, rewards, or bonuses.			

1. How many are dos and how many are don'ts?

_____

_____

_____

2. Identify the three don'ts that you would like to turn into dos.

_____

_____

_____

3. Identify the behaviors that you do sometimes and explain why you do so.

_____

_____

_____

Moving On

Overview

This is the final stage of engagement through the employee's career. At this time, she has decided to leave the current career and embark in a new one, returning to the Just Beginning stage elsewhere; or she's decided to leave the workforce altogether. This employee believes that she has reached the maximum level of productivity that she could attain, so she is ready to leave. She also could be engaged or disengaged from the company or from you.

As the employee gets ready to end her relationship with the company, she will focus her energy on preparing for that important transition in as many aspects of her life as possible. Some companies may provide support services for these employees such as emotional or financial counseling, while others may not do so. Similarly, some employees may choose not to use employer-sponsored services even if they are available. You as a manager could provide valuable assistance to your employee by directing her to those services when the opportunity arises and assuming that the employee explicitly expresses her intentions to leave the company with sufficient lead time for you to do something besides planning the typical farewell event.

This stage marks an important juncture for your team because they will need to adjust to the absence of the departing team member. Therefore, you will need to pay special attention to any possible signs of changes in employee engagement in the members of the team (stayers) as a result of this departure to make sure that you continue fostering their engagement with the company and with you.

LISTEN UP!

Always keep in mind the needs of those who stay. They will keep the business running.

Before we continue our discussion of the Moving On stage, we would like you to identify in which stage of their careers your employees are.

Now it's your turn.

Who is in the Moving On stage? List the names of those employees who are in this stage in Worksheet 8.7.

Worksheet 8.7   Employees in the Moving On Stage

	EMPLOYEE NAMES
MOVING ON	

Drivers

The employee who reaches this stage may be already disengaged and focused on leaving the company, but we have some suggestions for you as a manager to consider. Please remember that you will be working simultaneously with the employee who is in the Moving On stage and with other employees who may be in other stages of engagement and who will be staying (stayers); you will need to be ready to address everyone's needs. Specifically, we urge you to maintain communication with all employees, pay special attention to all details about performance management, and be aware of what's going on, because others will be particularly sensitive to everything that you do or the company does. By focusing on these two crucial drivers of employee engagement during this transition—namely communication and performance management—you will be better positioned to continue to foster engagement after the team reorganizes itself. At the same time, we encourage you to be realistic about what you can do within the timeframe that you have available. The employee who is leaving may have given you sufficient formal advanced notice to act accordingly; too much time, which delays closing the relationship; or too little time to do what is customary in your organization. You must therefore respond quickly and accordingly.

Employee Behaviors

The following is a list of some employee behaviors that you may observe during the Moving On stage. These behaviors will vary depending on the reason why the employee is Moving On.

» Shows signs of disengagement versus "super engagement" with the company and manager.

» Participates as little as possible or too much in the organization and its events.

» Talks about the past even more often than before and tries to focus on positive experiences.

» Searches for meaning of the past in conversations with others.

» May communicate optimistic or pessimistic expectations about the future.

» Tries to make amends with those employees with whom he has unresolved issues.

» Maintains minimal level of personal belongings at the workplace.

» Distributes personal items among co-workers.

Now it's your turn.

Select which behaviors from this list you have observed among the employees who are in the Moving On stage in Worksheet 8.8.

Worksheet 8.8 Behaviors Observed From Employees in Moving On Stage

BEHAVIORS	EMPLOYEE NAMES		
Shows signs of disengagement versus "super engagement" with the company and manager.			
Participates as little as possible or too much in the organization and its events.			
Talks about the past even more often than before and tries to focus on positive experiences.			
Searches for meaning of the past in conversations with others.			
May communicate optimistic or pessimistic expectations about the future.			
Tries to make amends with those employees with whom he has unresolved issues.			
Maintains minimal level of personal belongings at the workplace.			
Distributes personal items among co-workers.			

Manager Dos and Don'ts

Here are some examples of what you should and should not do when an employee is in the Moving On stage. Remember that you will need to adjust your behaviors based on the reason that the employee is Moving On.

Dos

» Value contributions.

» Facilitate the transition out of the organization or position.

» Ensure that knowledge gets transferred.

- » Show empathy.

- » Use your interpersonal skills.

- » Be respectful and show respect.

- » Communicate and listen.

Don'ts

- » Dismiss the employee's role and place in history.

- » Disregard any proposals from the employee about the transition or knowledge transfer.

- » Minimize the importance of contributions.

- » Miss an opportunity to recognize and reward.

- » Gossip around.

- » Change everything.

LISTEN UP!

Let your employees grieve. It's all about the "I."

Now it's your turn.

Worksheet 8.9 presents a behavior self-assessment for you to identify those behaviors that you have displayed or that you display typically. Place a check mark on the right column to indicate if you display those behaviors, you do not display them, or you display them sometimes.

Worksheet 8.9   Manager Behavior Self-Assessment: Moving On Stage

BEHAVIOR	YES	NO	SOMETIMES
DOS:			
Value contributions.			
Facilitate the transition out of the organization or position.			
Ensure that knowledge gets transferred.			
Show empathy.			
Use your interpersonal skills.			
Be respectful and show respect.			
Communicate and listen.			
DON'TS:			
Dismiss the employee's role and place in history.			
Disregard any proposals from the employee about the transition or knowledge transfer.			
Minimize the importance of contributions.			
Miss an opportunity to recognize and reward.			
Gossip around.			
Change everything.			

1.   How many are dos and how many are don'ts?

_____

_____

_____

_____

_____

2. Identify the three don'ts that you would like to turn into dos.

_____

_____

_____

3. Identify the behaviors that you do sometimes and explain why you do so.

_____

_____

_____

KEY POINTS AND TAKEAWAYS FOR PART III

- My Career "I" Path, yours and theirs, affect each other.
- Respect the future Career "I" Path of the employees.
- Avoid false promises or commitments.
- Benefits, image, and environment are grounds for Getting Settled.
- Address positive and negative reactions to newcomers in the team.
- Ensure rewards related to growth and development are available as promised.
- Steadiness and stability are key in Getting Settled.
- Employees generally accept reality "as is" in Getting Settled.
- Career opportunities are important in Looking for More. Watch out for potential misunderstandings.
- In Riding the Tide, employees seek stability and ward off obsolescence.
- Maintain focus and show respect.
- Extremes are common in Mission Accomplished: either extreme of satisfaction or dissatisfaction.
- Be ready to act quickly and accordingly—you may have too little or too much time to respond upon learning that someone is Moving On.

PART IV

Bringing It All Together

Introduction

We already discussed how an employee's engagement experience varies depending on his step in the Engagement "I" Path as well as on his Career "I" Path. Throughout these chapters we described typical employee behaviors and introduced a series of "manager's dos and don'ts" after our discussion of each step or stage. The last two chapters of the book will help you to reflect on what you have learned and discovered about employee engagement and to delineate your action plan for the future. In chapter 9, we guide you to think about your role as a model for your employees' engagement and to ponder on how you are living up to standards. After all, "engagement is all about the I" and your efforts will have a higher payoff when you are consistent in what you say and what you do. We also suggest what you can do to be a more effective role model. In chapter 10, the last chapter of this book, we take you through a process that you can use to turn your new ideas about how you as a manager can foster employee engagement into concrete actions for the benefit of your employees, your company, and you. Everything will make more sense and you will be ready to take action after cutting through the noise.

From Generic to Individual Attention: Are You Practicing What You Preach?

Overview

In this chapter, we will focus on you as an engagement role model for your employees. Of course, everybody wants to be a role model, but what are the requirements?

As you make decisions about what you will do to be a role model, we encourage you to consider that your employees need to feel safe in an environment where they are part of something bigger than themselves. As their manager, you can make a difference in what Erickson and Gratton (2010) call the "signature experience" of each employee through your modeling.

LISTEN UP!

Being a role model is living up to the standards.

Manager as a Role Model

We acknowledge the multiple demands on your time and attention as a manager; however, your most important responsibility is being a role model for employee engagement. As a role model you should:

» Demonstrate consistency in words, actions, behaviors, and language.

» Be aware of others' perceptions of yourself and shape those perceptions as much as possible.

» Comply with rules and regulations.

» Be a policy advocate.

» Understand that everything you do is tied to the organization's vision, mission, values, strategies, and objectives as well as to the company's value proposition leading to business results.

» Shape the individual employee engagement experience.

» Know your role.

» Be knowledgeable of employees' roles and responsibilities.

» Be the voice of the management.

> **LISTEN UP!**
>
> A role model is someone whose behavior is followed by others.

What a great responsibility. Your employees are a reflection of you. Remember: Good intentions aren't enough.

We invite you to keep in mind that "one size does not fit all" when making decisions about how to foster employee engagement among your employees as a role model. Therefore, you will need to recognize and celebrate differences as well as similarities in your team. Role models demonstrate achievements. As part of your role, you can be fair and professional; that does not mean that you are a "yes" person.

It is now time to look at your characteristics as a role model.

LISTEN UP!
Your employees will test you.

Now it's your turn.

The Manager's Role Model Self-Assessment presented in Worksheet 9.1 contains a list of characteristics typically associated with being a role model. Please indicate which ones describe you as "yes," and for those that do not describe you indicate as a "no" under the appropriate column.

For those characteristics that you identified as "yes," please indicate if you believe that you still need to improve on that characteristic. Likewise, for those characteristics that you identified as "no," please identify if you need to acquire them if they are important for you.

Worksheet 9.1   Manager's Role Model Self-Assessment

CHARACTERISTIC	YES	NEEDS IMPROVEMENT	NO	NEED TO ACQUIRE
Corporate citizen				
Strong business sense				
Goal-oriented				
Knowledgeable				
Honor your reputation				
Integrity				
Focus				

CHARACTERISTIC	YES	NEEDS IMPROVEMENT	NO	NEED TO ACQUIRE
Competitiveness				
Persistence				
Listening (hearing what they are not saying)				
Discipline				
Able to provide structure				
Respect				
Avoid fear				
Supportive				
Promote learning and development				
Measure return-on-investment (ROI)				
Aware of things that people value				
Able to or willing to change				
Value diversity				

For how many characteristics did you place a mark under "yes"? How many of those that you marked as "yes" are also identified as "needs improvement"? For how many did you do so under "no"? How many of those that you marked as "no" are also identified as "need to acquire"? Tabulate your answers in Worksheet 9.2.

Worksheet 9.2   **Results of Manager's Role Model Self-Assessment**

YES	NEEDS IMPROVEMENT	NO	NEED TO ACQUIRE

Now we will look at those characteristics that you identified as "yes" and also "needs improvement" in Worksheet 9.3. Select the three characteristics that you believe are the most important for you and the three actions that you will take to do so.

Worksheet 9.3   Top Three Characteristics to Improve

NEEDS IMPROVEMENT	ACTIONS

Now let's take another look at those characteristics that you identified as "no" and also "need to acquire" in Worksheet 9.4. Select the three characteristics that you believe are the most important for you to acquire and the three actions that you will take to do so.

Worksheet 9.4   Top Three Characteristics to Acquire

NEED TO ACQUIRE	ACTIONS

This exercise is a starting point for you to strengthen your position as a role model for engagement for your employees. Remember that, most importantly, you show how engaged you are with your company by demonstrating consistency in everything you do and say with conviction as you spend time with your team and your employees.

LISTEN UP!

Someone is always looking.

Based on your answers to the previous questions, you may want to invest some time on your own development, perhaps through participation in management or supervisor programs or other activities. By doing so, you would also be setting an example of your interest in continual professional improvement for your team. In other words: being a role model.

Characteristics of a Role Model

We will now discuss those characteristics that we believe are most significant for you, to be not only a manager, but also a role model of engagement.

Listening (Hearing What They Are Not Saying)

The key to establishing good relationships with your employees and with others is listening carefully to what they say as well as to what they do not say. By doing so, you will obtain valuable information about them as individuals and as employees; information about these two deeply intertwined dimensions will help you to guide your efforts to meet their needs and reach your engagement goals. As you listen to your employees, you will be modeling this important skill while you determine what resources they need and what obstacles you need to remove.

Listening (hearing what they are not saying) will also allow you to calibrate what you can realistically delegate to them so that you can dedicate your energies to other tasks. By gradually delegating tasks to them, you will promote their ownership and empowerment of the final product, which in turn will typically bring increasing levels of engagement as a result of a sense of accomplishment.

You will be able to listen to your employees only if you create a climate of trust where they can speak freely and confidentially without fearing negative repercussions if they disagree with you on a particular issue. Only then will you be able to really learn about them and from them, and to find opportunities to provide them with helpful feedback and coaching. Soon they will be practicing their listening skills with each other.

Communication

All exchanges with employees entail some type of communication. We reiterate the importance of consistency in messages as well as of establishing a climate of openness and trust where employees feel comfortable discussing multiple issues with you as a manager. As a role model, you will demonstrate the behaviors that you would like your employees to display, such as waiting for them to finish their thoughts, taking turns, explaining ideas clearly, using appropriate language, conveying emotions appropriately, showing appreciation, and disagreeing respectfully. Your nonverbal communication, including voice quality, physical gestures, and space use, should be congruent with your verbal communication at all times so that they feel valued. Again, your employees will be paying attention to everything that you convey.

As you diversify the available ways in which your employees complete their work, you will also need to diversify the means that you use to communicate with them. We encourage you to use available technologies and to tailor their use to the individual needs and experiences of your employees based on what works best for each one of them. For instance, some members of your team would prefer face-to-face communication, in person or virtually, while others are perfectly comfortable with short emails and text messages; still others may prefer telephone calls. The key point here is to communicate frequently using available means, using technology as an aid to increase productivity instead of something to use for its own sake.

LISTEN UP!

There is no way to
"not communicate."

Value Diversity

In today's workforce, diversity takes multiple forms. These include typical demographic characteristics such as age, gender, religion, veteran status, and ethnicity as well as socioeconomic status and educational level. They also include some characteristics that are not so typical, such as sexual orientation. You need to ensure that all of your employees are able to understand the value of individual uniqueness and how each one contributes to the overall success of the team as part of your day-to-day responsibilities. Most importantly, you need to demonstrate openness and inclusiveness to employees who have different characteristics in your everyday interactions with everyone so that all of them see you consistently "walking the talk." Remember that valuing diversity entails more than complying with the applicable laws.

LISTEN UP!

Valuing diversity is a way of life.

Knowledgeable

As a manager, you are a major source of information for your employees. Although it is not realistic to expect you to know everything about everything, it is reasonable to assume that you master your responsibilities. You should also be able to point others in the right direction to obtain the resources that they need. In the Information Age, at a very minimum, you will be expected to know where to find what you need to know.

Being knowledgeable also means knowing what you do not know, so that you can determine if it is important for you to learn it or not. If you decide that learning something is important, then you have multiple options to obtain that knowledge; we mention some of them in the context of learning and development activities to foster employee engagement in other chapters of this book. We invite you to keep in mind that you do not need to learn everything that you do not know; being selective about what you need to know will allow you to prioritize and focus your efforts.

Your employees will look up to you as a role model in terms of the knowledge that you have, how you use it, and how you show evidence that you have it or do not have it.

For instance, you may be a subject matter expert on a topic who openly shares information with others, or you could only share information with others on a need-to-know basis. Which one of these two types of subject matter experts do you want them to be? Remember that you are always sending messages to others and your employees will do as you do much more than as you say.

LISTEN UP!
Keep raising the knowledge bar.

Respect

In today's work environment, the quality of interactions and relationships with others will be what helps you to get to where you need and want to be. All members of a company share a common purpose: to fulfill the mission and obtain business results from their roles; everyone's contribution is important. In the end, you obtain results by skillfully working through others; it's all about treating others how you would like them to treat you. Make sure that your employees see you as someone who values and respects others at all times and not only when you need something. Be keenly aware of how others perceive how you treat others, especially those who perform tasks that may not have as much apparent value in the company. Your employees will be more likely to respect you and each other, and become more engaged to you, if they see you behaving consistently.

LISTEN UP!

Be consistent in how you show your respect for others. Your employees will notice.

Supportive

One of your many responsibilities as a manager is to encourage others to become the best that they can be. To do this, you may have to step out of the way so that they acquire new skills while making mistakes. As learners, your employees will feel vulnerable and may be afraid to seem incompetent to you. At some point, you will need to come to terms with the value of allowing others to learn in whichever way they do, because in the end, your team and the company will benefit. You will also need to find a way to convey that you are there for them, you will do your best to provide resources and information, as well as, perhaps more importantly, offer a shoulder to lean on without passing judgment.

There will be other times when your employees will be facing personal situations that may require you to be flexible in work-related issues, such as scheduling. You may need to handle expressions of raw emotions or simply allow them some space to solve whatever situation they are encountering. In the end, your respect for privacy and empathy will take you a long way.

Your employees will look up to you, as a manager, to help them in situations such as the ones that we just mentioned. In addition, they will pay particular attention to how you do what you need to do and will, very likely, replicate what you do when it is time for them to assist someone else, which could mean prioritizing someone else's needs over their own. That someone could be you.

Focus

In today's fast-paced work environment, we encounter plenty of distractions as a result of competing priorities and messages. As a manager, you face particular challenges as a consequence of the multiple simultaneous demands placed on you and, very likely, the number of these demands will not diminish any time soon.

Although many tout the benefits of multitasking, many others value the capacity to focus on a task or a person at a particular point in time. Obtaining a sense of accomplishment after finishing a series of tasks becomes a source of motivation to continue with other tasks. Receiving the full attention of someone during a meeting reinforces one's value.

Your employees will easily notice how you organize your work and how you interact with them.

- » Do you establish priorities?
- » How well do you manage your time?
- » Do you try to answer emails during individual meetings with them?
- » Are you always in a hurry and cannot seem to get anything done on time?

If you do something and expect them to do something else, you will lack congruence in your behavior; their engagement will be affected accordingly.

Persistence

This characteristic is closely related to focus. As you decide what you will do and what your goals are, you will need to spend time and attention on the relevant tasks. At times, you may not obtain the results that you want as soon as you would like to, so you may need to dedicate more efforts to what you are doing. You may also experience frustration if you do not get what you want when you want it, or if you don't experience extreme levels of happiness when you finally do.

Your determination to complete what you are doing or to see something through until its logical conclusion will serve as an example to others to do the same, particularly in times when everything seems to have been due yesterday. Likewise, how you control your emotions—both negative and positive—will set a standard for your employees to react under comparable circumstances. If your employees see you follow through tasks with a positive attitude, they will be more likely to do the same when they face a challenging situation. Be consistent.

LISTEN UP!

Patience is always a virtue.

Able or Willing to Change

Some time ago, entering the workforce meant having one career in one company for many years until reaching the age of retirement. Back then, no one dreamed about reinventing himself several times in different careers or changing jobs and companies repeatedly. Since succeeding in today's workplace is all about handling change, you need to be able to or be willing to change to adapt and evolve. How would you respond to the following questions about your ability to change?

» Do you always follow the same routines and procedures to complete your work?

» Do you intend to remain in the same type of work for the rest of your career?

» Do you cringe at the thought of trying something new in your professional or your personal lives?

» Do you look for alternate and, perhaps more efficient, ways
to complete your work so that you can get different results?

» Are you willing to go out of your way as well as to spend time
and energy to acquire new skills and competencies?

» Do you see yourself in the future doing something that you
did not expect when you started your career?

Flexibility, flexibility, flexibility is what will help you to continue to make progress in your career and is what you need to convey to your employees. They need to be able to or be willing to change, particularly under times of company uncertainty. As you demonstrate this capability and show its benefits, your employees will see how this quality can benefit them and the company. Thus, they will very likely be more eager to go beyond what is expected of them. Remember that flexibility is not saying "yes" at all times.

LISTEN UP!
Knowing that you can adapt to
change builds self-confidence.

Aware of What People Value

As you interact with your employees, you will learn what is important for them professionally and personally. This information will be very useful for you—as a manager and as a role model—because it will allow you to address their particular needs at any given time. For example:

Ronald prefers to be addressed at work by his last name, Smith, instead of his first name. Karen dislikes the use of last names in the workplace. Address each one as he or she prefers. Be particularly careful with nicknames.

Kevin favors public recognitions. Jeff would rather receive a handwritten note from you for a job well done when no one else is present. Recognize Kevin in public and Jeff in private.

By paying attention to your employees as individuals beyond their role in your company, they will feel appreciated. Very likely, your employees will become more engaged because they will have a stronger emotional connection with you simply because "you noticed."

As your employees detect how you distinguish those differences without showing preferences for individuals in your team, they will also get to know you and each other at a deeper level. This knowledge will help them to work together better—particularly under stressful conditions where emotional reactions can create significant disruptions.

LISTEN UP!
Acknowledge the uniqueness of each employee.

Avoid Fear

Fear is one of the most paralyzing emotions that a human being can feel in the workplace. It is often the result of not knowing what will happen under conditions of perceived threat to something valuable. Let's see two examples.

Ruth could be afraid of losing her job as a result of a merger or an acquisition because it represents her only source of income. Under the circumstances, her anxiety may lead her to make mistakes that could lead to the undesired result.

Jason could be afraid of losing a coveted spot on a highly visible project that may mean potential career opportunities. By coming across as insecure and afraid, Jason may actually shortchange his chances of remaining in the project, thus actually limiting his options.

In both examples, fear is also the consequence of not having control over what is happening or could happen. You cannot afford to be paralyzed by fear because you won't be able to see clearly what you need to do. When someone is afraid, she cannot focus on what can be controlled, thus she loses valuable time and energy and projects an inappropriate image of herself.

You cannot become emotionally disconnected and disengaged as a result of your fear. Therefore, you need to avoid fear, or handle it, by increasing your sense of control over what you can control and by finding ways to influence what you can influence. You need to keep your emotions under control so that your employees do not assume that reality is even worse than it actually is and start taking actions, such as leaving the company prematurely.

LISTEN UP!

If you remain calm, your employees will be calm too.

Promote Learning and Development

We have news for you. Even though you are a manager, you still need to find ways to continue to learn and grow as a professional. You need to attend company-mandated or sponsored learning and development events such as formal classroom-based trainings. At other times you may be required to take online courses. Or you may be given the option to receive coaching or mentoring from an internal or external resource.

You may be reluctant to attend those events or participate in those activities. Perhaps you would rather continue doing what you are doing than stop in the middle of the morning to attend a lecture. Maybe you would prefer to take those online courses from the comfort of your home, but this is not an option given the regulated environment in which you work. Possibly you do not see the value of having someone who can help you to address some blind spots that may be holding you back in your work.

If you do not participate in those events or take those courses when they are required, or even accept support from a well-intentioned mentor or coach, you will be conveying to your employees that you do not really believe in learning and development. Pause for a moment.

Think about how your employees will feel about complying with the same requests—will they be open to the new experiences or will they find ways to avoid participating because they also have a lot of work to do?

Visualize what could happen if your employees do not take those opportunities seriously.

Your company could be subject to fines and lawsuits under the unfortunate event of accidents caused by employees who were not properly trained to fulfill their responsibilities. Your company could simply lose revenue as a result of not having people who are up to date in the latest trends of their industry.

You and your employees will only have a future if you prepare for the challenges that the future will bring. When your employees see the value of learning and development activities and how they benefit from them, they will feel valued; because in the end, what they learn is for them to keep. If you attend those events with them, they will be inspired to continue learning. Make a point of doing so.

LISTEN UP!

Learning and development is an investment in the future—others' and yours.

We have underscored the importance of you as a manager to serve as an engagement role model for your employees. We have also discussed the most salient characteristics of that important function so that you can be aware of where you are and can make the necessary adjustments to become an even better role model.

For you to be their most effective role model, you need to know more about your own engagement level and how you are communicating that engagement level to your employees. In the next section, you will answer some questions that will help you to see where you are in your own engagement.

Now it's your turn.

The following questions that compose the Manager Engagement Self-Assessment presented in Worksheet 9.5 address specific components of your own engagement. Please indicate your answer to each one and include any examples of behaviors that show why you answered "yes," "no," or "don't know" under the column labeled "behaviors."

Worksheet 9.5   Manager Engagement Self-Assessment

QUESTION	YES	NO	DON'T KNOW	BEHAVIORS
Do I feel emotionally connected to my company?				
Do I feel emotionally connected to my team?				
Do I want to come to work every day?				
Are my values and the values of my company aligned?				
Do I believe in what my company stands for?				
Do I support my company in its mission?				
Do I believe that my company is true to its core values?				
Do I believe that my company supports its employees?				
Do I agree with my company's position in different topics?				
Do I agree with how my company presents itself to others?				
Do I support my company in its interactions with external stakeholders (for example, community)?				
Do I limit my involvement in my company to my job description?				

QUESTION	YES	NO	DON'T KNOW	BEHAVIORS
Do I expect my team to limit their involvement in my company to their job descriptions?				
Do I convey my commitment to my company through my actions and behaviors on the job?				
Do I convey my commitment to my company through my actions and behaviors outside of the workplace?				
Do I believe that my company provides opportunities for growth and development for all employees?				
Do I intend to continue belonging to my company for a long time?				
Am I willing to dedicate as much time and resources as my company needs to accomplish its goals?				
Do I feel fulfilled and energized with what I do at my company?				
Do I want to come to work every day because I enjoy what I do at my company?				
Do I feel valued for the work that I do?				
Do I have the tools that enable me to do my job?				
Would I be willing to continue belonging to my company if my pay and rewards were reduced?				
Does my manager inspire me?				
Would I recommend my company to others as a good place to work?				
Do I feel proud to tell people where I work?				
Have I always felt this way about my company?				

Count how many questions you answered with "yes," "no," or "don't know" and write the numbers in Worksheet 9.6.

Worksheet 9.6   Results of Manager Engagement Self-Assessment

YES	NO	DON'T KNOW

- » If you answered "yes" to between 13 and 17 questions, you seem to be solidly engaged with your company. You are doing fine, but should consider paying attention to those areas which you still need to address.

- » If you answered "yes" to 18 or more questions, you are highly engaged with your company. Congratulations! You should still review those questions to which you answered "no" and find out why. Once you do, you will be able to take action to turn those answers into "yes."

- » If you answered "no" to between 13 and 17 questions, you seem to be disengaged with the company. We invite you to think about why this is the case so that you can make the best possible decision for yourself and for the company. What is going on either at the company or in your life that is affecting your engagement with the company? Whatever is happening is, very likely, showing through your words and actions; and unless the reason is personal, others may soon become disengaged.

- » If you answered "no" to 18 or more questions, you seem to be highly disengaged with the company. This situation demands prompt and closer attention from you because your high level of disengagement will certainly have a negative effect on your employees. You may even consider seeking support from someone whom you trust to address whatever professional or personal situations you are facing so that you can solve them promptly.

» If your answer to most of the questions was "don't know," we invite you to look at those questions again and at the behaviors that you mentioned. Let's look at an example.

» If you answered "don't know" to "Do I convey my commitment to my organization through my actions and behaviors outside of the workplace?", what do you do when someone asks for information about your organization when you are running errands on the weekends? If you provide that information even though you are not working at that time, then you should change your answer to that question to "yes." If instead you ask them to look up the telephone number of the switchboard and call on Monday, you should change your answer to that question to "no."

Look at your answers. The patterns that you find in the information that you included in your answers will help you to see specific areas of your career that may be affecting your levels of engagement either positively or negatively. We invite you to consider what you still need to change or adjust to be an even better role model for your employees.

LISTEN UP!

Get what you need and take action. Every day.

Remember

» Go back to your results of the Role Model Self-Assessment (Worksheet 9.1).

» Review the results of your Engagement Self-Assessment.

» Get to know your employees.

» Model what you want to see in your employees.

» Determine if your challenge with employees is related to engagement or fit.

» Review and repeat.

KEY POINTS AND TAKEAWAYS

- Role models influence. You are being watched.
- You make a difference in your employees' level of engagement.
- Your most important responsibility is being a role model.
- Be consistent. You are shaping your employees' engagement.
- You show how engaged you are through everything that you do.
- Invest time in your own development.
- Listen to what they say and don't say. Create a climate of trust.
- Being knowledgeable means also knowing what you don't know.
- It's all about treating others how you would like them to treat you.
- Encourage others to be their best.
- Respect and privacy will take you a long way.
- You could multitask, but don't belittle.
- Convey your own flexibility to your employees.
- Confront fear.
- Prepare for the future: Practice and preach support for learning and development.

CHAPTER 10:

Next Steps and Action Planning in Employee Engagement

Introduction

In the beginning of this book we invited you to join us in the journey toward employee engagement. Our journey together is about to end, but yours is just beginning. Let's review what we have done and show you some options for where to go next.

We shared with you our definition of engagement based on our research and on our experience as practitioners. We presented those elements existing in organizations that propel engagement (drivers of engagement). We discussed statistics and trends to place our work and your company in a broader context. We explained the impact of employee engagement on the business and on employees. We defined organizational culture as well as individual differences within a culture and their role in employee engagement. We introduced the Engagement "I" Path's steps and the Career "I" Path's stages, with specific examples of employee behaviors and suggestions for what you should do and avoid as a manager. We expounded on your role as a manager throughout the book, but, most importantly, as a role model of engagement for your employees. We guided you to think about your company and about your own experiences and how those have an impact on your employees, by asking you to complete multiple exercises and to reflect about what we had just shared with you. We sprinkled each chapter with the "Listen Up!" notes, with ideas for you to stop and consider, and ended each chapter or section with Key Points and Take-aways for you to remember their major ideas. As we said before, "this is your book" and "someone is always watching."

After reading all the other chapters (or those of most interest to you), and completing all the exercises and questionnaires that we included here, you have a different understanding of what employee engagement is all about. You also have collected valuable information about yourself and about your employees that will complement or supplement any information about employee engagement that your company has obtained and given you. You may also be asking yourself: Now what?

We will now help you answer that question.

Start Now and Think Ahead

We believe in using what you learn as soon as you learn it, so we invite you to think about what you can do about employee engagement starting tomorrow. As a reminder, everything that you do should be linked with business results.

Start now.

> » Set up some time in your agenda to continue to learn more about the topic or about specific topics that caught your attention in this book.

> » Start telling others (be specific!) about what you just learned to get them interested and involved in your efforts. Begin to build momentum.

Then, look at next week.

> » Gather more information about employee engagement in your company.

> » Spend more quality time with each one of your employees.

> » Schedule a meeting with a C-level executive who could serve as the sponsor for your initiatives.

> » Identify company-wide initiatives to foster employee engagement. Become their champion for your employees.

See what you could do next month.

» Complete the assessments included in this book for your employees and compare their results and your results.

» Collect data to prepare your action plan.

» Identify those top three dos and don'ts from either the Engagement "I" Path or Career "I" Path with which you will work and split them throughout the year.

» Help someone from your team to learn something new. Push experience.

Anything further in the future than next month is more an issue of action planning, which is the topic that we discuss in the next section of this chapter.

Action Planning

You may have heard this term before, but, just in case: We define *action planning* as a deliberate effort to organize what steps you will take to address the needs that you have already identified in your company, to accomplish a specific goal. Bringing it home, you have the goal of increasing engagement among your employees and, perhaps, among employees elsewhere in your company. Maybe you already belong to a division-wide or company-wide task force chartered to increase employee engagement and that is why you chose to read this book. Action planning will help you to translate your results into specific steps and activities that can have a direct impact on your employees and on your business.

Before we get into the details, let's differentiate between strategy and activity. A strategy is the overall approach that you will follow to accomplish something. For example: You will have a participatory strategy to increase employee engagement because you want your employees to feel that their opinions matter.

In contrast, an activity is what you actually do to reach the employees and allow them to feel that their opinions matter. For example: You rotate who will design and lead your team meetings. It's a way to share the work and prepare others for other roles.

We are glad that you have been reading our book, but we understand completely the need to do something with data and results, particularly when it comes to employee engagement. Collecting employee data and feedback and then choosing to disregard it or to do something completely different from what the data suggest can be totally counterproductive. In fact, in our experience, such decisions can lead to disengagement as employees lose faith in the process and become skeptical about the true value those managers at all levels (yes, including you) place on them as well as on their opinions. You can bet on, at the very least, having lower participation rates in future surveys and interviews and minimal collaboration in any initiatives because they may feel that their opinions are not valued or that senior management already knows what they will do, so the survey was just "to pretend to hear employees."

In short, sound action planning and targeted frequent communication emphasizing what you learned and what you are doing about it will take you a long way toward promoting employee engagement in your company. A reminder: Days only have a finite number of hours and you still have to perform your role as a manager, so you do not have to do everything at once.

We promise to keep it simple.

Steps to Action Planning

We see the steps in action planning as the steps on a ladder as Figure 3 presents. We will delve into each one of those steps separately, starting with the first step or the bottom of the staircase.

It all begins with your definition of employee engagement, because this definition is the foundation of what you will do. We invite you to go back to your definition and to your company's definition; consider revising your definition based on what you learned throughout the book. Take your time.

After you review your definition and your company's definition of employee engagement, look for similarities and differences between them. Examine the data that you have available about yourself and about your employees.

Here is where any employee surveys come in handy as well as the results of the questions and questionnaires that you completed in other chapters of this book. See what your data tell you and how your definition and your data match. What is missing?

Figure 3   Steps in Action Planning

Which one will you tackle first? Yes, priorities are the next step. You need to determine what to do first, second, third, and so on. Just like you do when you decide how you will organize your work every day, consider what is critical, what is important, and what is nice to have. Connect them to the priorities of the business.

After you establish your priorities, you will need to define goals to address those priorities and to establish metrics. We invite you to be specific and to quantify those goals as much as possible. You may want to use the SMART (Specific, Measurable, Attainable, Realistic, and Timely) model. For example, say "increase employee engagement scores by 5 percent by next survey" instead of "increase employee engagement."

Now you need to look at what activities you will do to meet those goals. Let's say that you decide to communicate more, and more often as a means to "increase employee engagement scores by 5 percent by next survey." Again, make it specific. For example, say, "hold four quarterly meetings with all employees" instead of "have more meetings with all employees." Or, "publish employee newsletter monthly" instead of "publish employee newsletter."

After you define your activities, you need to determine the timeframe in which you will complete them and who will complete them. For example, you may want to hold quarterly meetings in March, June, September, and December. If you want to increase employee participation, you may decide that you will plan and conduct the meeting that will take place in March, while Pamela will do the same for June's meeting, George will take care of September's meeting, and Alex will handle December's meeting.

The next step will be to execute your activities. For example, did you complete them as scheduled? Why or why not? Did you have to change any resources to complete them?

You also need to measure the results of each one of the activities. Relax—you do not need to come up with complicated questionnaires to do this. A simple evaluation form with a few basic questions would be an appropriate start; such as: What did you like best/least about (the activity)? What would you do differently? Should we continue to have activities like this one in the future? You may also ask your employees to share their thoughts as an item on a meeting's agenda.

After you measure your results, you need to act on what you learn from those results and, very likely, revise your plan accordingly. Yes, it's time to go back to the drawing board of action planning. For example, if your survey respondents said that the quarterly departmental meetings are not useful because they are too long and do not allow time for valuable interactions between employees, you may want to consider what to do with them. Eliminating those meetings may not be the best idea, but you may want to redesign the meetings and mentor the employees who will plan and execute those meetings while they learn what they need to do.

Of course, your life will be easier when you articulate your plan on a document that you can use to track your progress. In the next section we present exactly such a tool.

LISTEN UP!
Focus on what you can change; live with what you can't.

A Tool to Set Up Your Action Plan

The best solution is usually the simplest solution, so we suggest the following structure for your action plan. You can use either a regular table created using word processing or a spreadsheet. Worksheet 10.1 presents a sample for you to begin to put your thoughts in writing. We will discuss each one of the different sections of the table separately.

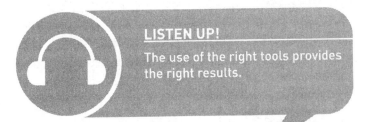

LISTEN UP!
The use of the right tools provides the right results.

Worksheet 10.1 Sample Template for Action Plan

GOAL: INCREASE EMPLOYEE ENGAGEMENT BY 5 PERCENT BY THE NEXT SURVEY						
Action 1: Communication.						
WHAT WILL WE DO?	HOW WILL WE DO IT?	WHO'S RESPONSIBLE FOR DOING IT?	WHEN DO WE NEED TO DO IT?	WILL WE MEASURE WHAT WE DID?	HOW MUCH WILL THIS COST US?	PROGRESS NOTES
Publish quarterly newsletter	Design the newsletter	Patrick, Lea, and Sam	March, June, September, December	Yes/No	30 hours	
	Collect writings from employees		Two months before publishing	Yes/No	23 hours	
	Revise writings		One month before publishing	Yes/No	8 hours	
	Prepare draft		Day 5	Yes/No	4 hours	
	Review draft		Day 10	Yes/No	3 hours	
	Publish		Day 20	Yes/No	2 hours + $200	
	Distribution		Day 25	Yes/No	2 hours	

Let's look at what you should include under each column.

Goal: Write which specific employee engagement goal you will address. Yes, you may have only one goal but many actions to address it; or many goals and many actions to address each goal. We said we would keep this simple, so we will use one goal with one action in our example.

Action 1: Write what general action you will take. Think about general areas, such as communication, learning and development, special projects, or senior management.

What will we do? Describe each activity that you will complete related to your action. Remember to include various activities depending on the needs of each one of your employees as well as of your team. Incorporate some learning and development activities and optimize available resources throughout your company. Personalization works.

How will we do it? Describe each step that you need to complete to execute each activity. Break it down into manageable chunks, preferably of less than a week.

Who's responsible for doing it? Who will be completing each step or the entire activity? You do not need to do everything yourself; it's time to delegate and develop others. Social integration develops good relationships.

When do we need to do it? This is your timeframe to complete the activity. Be as specific as you can with the dates. Most importantly, make sure that they are realistic considering all the other demands of your role as a manager.

Will we measure what we did? You can obtain useful information from very simple indicators. For example, you can see if a task was completed with a statement like: "activity completed yes/no;" or how participants responded to an activity by asking: "Should we do (name of activity) again?"

How much will this cost us? You need to determine the costs of the activities in terms of time, resources, and funding. Based on this information, you will be able to make the best decisions about which activities will be best suited to reach your goals. You will also be able to seek any additional resources that you may need. Remember to convert person-hours to cost per hour even when depending on regular employees as resources for your activities.

Progress notes: Write any comments about what is happening and any details that you may wish to remember later. For example, "Activity X was postponed because priorities changed."

After establishing your priorities and putting together your action plan, you are ready to begin to execute your plan. Most importantly, you as a manager are now ready to be a stronger employee engagement role model. We said it: It's an ending and a beginning.

We will close this chapter with some key points for you to remember and some takeaways for you to review what you learned by reading this book.

KEY POINTS AND TAKEAWAYS

- Use what you learn as soon as you learn it.
- Link everything that you do to business results.
- Tell others about what you learned and begin to build momentum.
- Become a champion of employee engagement initiatives for your employees.
- Help others to learn something new.
- Act on results and feedback quickly. They will notice.
- Remember engagement is individual.
- Role model learning and development. Get others involved.
- Seek what is meaningful to your employees individually and as a group.

LISTEN UP!

Respect. Trust.
Performance management.

Final Thoughts

This chapter marks an ending and a beginning for you as a manager and for us as authors. We wish that our paths will cross again as we continue to learn about employee engagement and to build on what we shared with you throughout these pages. We encourage you to:

» Belong.

» Learn.

» Be remembered.

» Be engaged.

The question is the answer. Enjoy the journey.

Norma and Wanda

References

Aon Hewitt. (2012). *Making Employee Engagement Happen: Best Practices from Best Employers,* http://www.aon.com/human-capital-consulting/thought-leadership/talent_mgmt/2012_Making_Employee_Engagement_Happen_Best_Practices_Best_Employers_White_Paper.jsp.

Aon Hewitt. (2011). *Trends in Global Employee Engagement,* http://www.aon.com/attachments/thought-leadership/Trends_Global_Employee_Engagement_Final.pdf.

Harter, Jim. (2012). *Mondays Not So "Blue" for Engaged Employees.* Gallup, http://www.gallup.com/poll/155924/Mondays-Not-Blue-Engaged-Employees.aspx.

Hewitt Associates. (2010). *Employee Engagement in Turbulent Times: How Other Organizations Are Performing.* www.hewitt.com.

Thomas, K.W. (2009). *Intrinsic Motivation at Work: What Really Drives Employee Engagement,* 2nd edition. San Francisco, CA: Berrett-Koehler Publishers, Inc.

Towers Watson. (2012). 2012 *Global Workforce Study, Engagement At Risk: Driving Strong Performance in a Volatile Global Environment,* www.towerswatson.com.

World at Work. (2011). *Total Rewards Model: A Framework for Strategies to Attract, Motivate and Retain Employees,* http://www.worldatwork.org/waw/adimLink?id = 28330.

About the Authors

Norma Dávila

Norma Dávila has dedicated her career to develop others in industries as diverse as banking, technology, pharmaceuticals, retail, utilities and education. She is a hands-on consultant in organizational development and training who designs and implements change management, capacity building, and e-learning strategies. She prepares internal organizational capacity for different roles through coaching. Norma provides outplacement support, designs employee handbooks, challenges operational processes, and prepares grant proposals, among other services. Her consulting practice also includes leadership development and talent management programs. She is known for her flexibility in working with her clients to address their needs and partnering to find the best solution to their challenges. Norma is certified as a Project Management Professional (PMP) and a Senior Professional in Human Resources (SPHR). She earned her bachelor's degree in psychology at Yale University and her master's and doctoral degrees in psychology at the University of Chicago.

Wanda Piña-Ramírez

Wanda Piña-Ramírez is an enthusiastic advocate of selecting and developing talent for business success who has held various roles in human resources in industries such as hospitality, tourism, telecommunications, petrochemicals, retail, and government in the United States, the Caribbean Region, and Puerto Rico. Her clients range from multinational corporations to small and midsize businesses for corporate reorganizations, contract negotiations, budget development and management, human resources administration, business management, and training, among other services. Wanda is certified as a Coach (CCC) from the University of Puerto Rico at Río Piedras, as a

Practitioner in Neurolinguistic Programming and Applied Kinesiology by the International NLP Trainers Association, and as a Human Resources Administrator by the Escuela Avanzada de Administración de Recursos Humanos y Legislación Laboral de Puerto Rico. She serves as an Advisory Board Member of the School of Business Administration of the University of Puerto Rico at Bayamón. Wanda received the Training and Development Professional Award of the Puerto Rico chapter of the American Society for Training & Development in 2011.

Norma and Wanda are active members of the Puerto Rico chapter of the American Society for Training & Development where Wanda served as president in 2010 and Norma served as president in 2012. Both are very involved in the Society for Human Resources Management, where they have held various roles in the Puerto Rico chapter and served as subject matter experts for the national association. Both are certified as Development Dimensions International (DDI) facilitators. As friends and colleagues for several years, Norma and Wanda synergized their talents by founding The Human Factor Consulting Group.

Index

A

Ability or willingness to change,
   196–197
Acronyms, 30
Action planning
   activities in, 214–215
   definition of, 209
   employee engagement through,
      210
   priority setting, 212, 216
   process model of, 211
   steps in, 210-212
   template for, 214–215
   tool for setting up action plan,
      212–216
Activity
   in action plan, 214–215
   execution of, 212
   measuring the results of, 212–213
   strategy versus, 209
Age of employees, 19
Aon Hewitt, 19, 23
Attitudes, 25–26
Autonomy, 10

B

Behavior self-assessments.
   See Manager behavior
   self-assessments
Beliefs, 27
Bodyguard, 43, 45

Brand alignment, 14–15, 83–84
Branding, 56
Business, employee engagement
   impact on, 22–23

C

Career development, 12–13
Career "I" Path
   description of, 135–136
   Getting Settled stage. See Getting
      Settled stage
   Just Beginning stage. See Just
      Beginning stage
   Looking for More stage. See
      Looking for More stage
   Mission Accomplished stage.
      See Mission Accomplished stage
   Moving On stage. See Moving
      On stage
   process model of, 137
   Riding the Tide stage. See Riding
      the Tide stage
Career opportunities, 84–85
Career potential, 84–85
Change, 196–197
Comfort zone, 135
Communication
   description of, 10
   employee engagement
      through, 210
   in Getting Settled stage, 148

manager, 74, 94
methods of, 191
in Moving On stage, 175
nonverbal, 191
by role model, 191
Critical Incidents turning point
career opportunities, 84–85
career potential, 84–85
description of, 53
drivers of, 83–85
emotional reactions to, 84
employee behaviors in, 86–88
information about, 82–83
manager dos and don'ts in, 88–89
overview of, 80–83
total rewards, 85
types of, 80–81

D

Decline step
description of, 53
drivers of, 102–103
employee behaviors in, 103–104
employees in, 102
manager dos and don'ts in,
105–106
overview of, 101–102
Demographic factors, 19–20
Diversity, 188
Drivers
brand alignment, 14–15, 83–84
career development, 12–13
of Critical Incidents turning point,
83–85
of Decline step, 102–103
external incentives, 13
financial incentives, 13
of Getting Settled stage, 146
of Growth step, 94–95

intrinsic motivation, 11
of Just Beginning stage, 141–142
leadership, 11
of Looking for More stage,
153–154
manager-employee relationship, 10
of Mission Accomplished stage,
167–168
of Moving On stage, 174–175
organizational image, 13–14,
83–84
performance management, 11–12
of Re-engagement or Disengagement turning point, 123–124
of Riding the Tide stage, 160–161
of Stable step, 74
of Starting Out step, 56–57
of Stay or Leave turning point,
112–113
of Testing the Waters step, 65–66

E

Education level, 19
Emotional component, 9–10, 13
Emotions, 196
Employee(s)
appreciation for, 196
employee engagement impact on,
23–24
expectations of, 28–29
growth and development
opportunities for, 12
highly engaged, 23
as learners, 192
personal beliefs of, 28
personal issues faced by, 194–195
professional, 20
well-being of, 23

Employee behaviors
  in Critical Incidents turning point,
    86–88
  in Decline step, 103–104
  in Getting Settled stage, 149–150
  in Growth step, 95–96
  in Just Beginning stage, 142–144
  in Looking for More stage,
    154–155
  in Mission Accomplished stage,
    168–169
  in Moving On stage, 175–176
  in Re-engagement or Disengage-
    ment turning point, 126–127
  in Riding the Tide stage, 161–163
  in Stable step, 74–76
  in Starting Out step, 57–58
  in Stay or Leave turning point,
    113–115
  in Testing the Waters step, 66–68
Employee engagement
  definition of, 9, 15
  drivers of. *See* Drivers
  facts of, 5–8
  foundation of, 9
  impact of, 22–24
  indicators of, 20
  myths of, 5–8
  rational component of, 9
Employee expectations, 153
Employee satisfaction, 141
Employee surveys, 210
Engagement "I" Path
  Critical Incidents turning
    point of. *See* Critical Incidents
    turning point
  Decline step of. *See* Decline step
  description of, 51
  Growth step of. *See* Growth step

  process model for, 51–52
  Re-engagement or Disengagement
    turning point. *See* Re-en-
    gagement or Disengagement
    turning point
  Starting Out step of. *See* Starting
    Out step
  Stay or Leave turning point. *See*
    Stay or Leave turning point
  Testing the Waters step of. *See*
    Testing the Waters step
Expectations, 28–29
External incentives, 13

F

Fear, 198–199
Financial incentives, 13
Flexibility, 153, 197
Focus, 195

G

Gender, 19
Getting Settled stage
  description of, 135
  drivers of, 148
  employee behaviors in, 149–150
  employees in, 147
  manager dos and don'ts in,
    150–151
  overview of, 147
Getting started, 208-209
Growth step
  description of, 53
  drivers of, 94–95
  employee behaviors in, 95–96
  employees in, 94
  manager dos and don'ts in, 96–98
  overview of, 93

H

Hewitt Associates, 23
Highly engaged employees, 23

I

"I," 9–10, 15–17
Incentives, 13, 154
Individuals, organizational culture
    and, 39–42
Intrinsic motivation, 11, 141

J

Job-related factors, 20
Just Beginning stage
    description of, 135
    drivers of, 141–142
    employee behaviors in, 142–144
    employees in, 141
    manager dos and don'ts in,
        144–145
    manager's role in, 140
    overview of, 139–140

K

Knowledge
    organizational culture and, 29–30
    of role model, 192–193

L

Language, 30–31
Leadership, 11
Learning and development, 199–200
Listening, 190–191
Looking for More stage
    description of, 135
    drivers of, 153–154
    employee behaviors in, 154–155

employees in, 153
manager dos and don'ts in,
    155–156
overview of, 152–153

M

Manager
    communication by, 74, 94
    engagement self-assessment for,
        199–200
    performance management
        systems, 74
    as role model. *See* Role model
    role of, in organizational culture,
        42–46
    team leadership by, 45
Manager behavior self-assessments
    in Critical Incidents turning point,
        90–92
    in Decline step, 107–108
    in Getting Settled stage, 151–152
    in Growth step, 98–101
    in Just Beginning stage, 145–147
    in Looking for More stage,
        156–158
    in Mission Accomplished stage,
        171–173
    in Moving On stage, 177–179
    in Re-engagement or Disengage-
        ment turning point, 129–131
    in Riding the Tide stage, 164–166
    in Stable step, 78–80
    in Starting Out step, 61–64
    in Stay or Leave turning point,
        118–121
    in Testing the Waters step, 69–71
Manager dos and don'ts
    in Critical Incidents turning point,
        88–89

in Decline step, 105–106
in Getting Settled stage, 150–1451
in Growth step, 96–98
in Just Beginning stage, 144–145
in Looking for More stage,
    155–156
in Mission Accomplished stage,
    170–171
in Moving On stage, 176–177
in Re-engagement or Disengage-
    ment turning point, 127–129
in Riding the Tide stage, 163–164
in Stable step, 76–77
in Starting Out step, 59–64
in Stay or Leave turning point,
    116–117
in Testing the Waters step, 68–71
Manager-employee relationship, 10
Materials, 34–35
Metrics, 23
Mission Accomplished stage
description of, 136
drivers of, 167–168
duration of, 168
employee behaviors in, 168–169
employees in, 167
manager dos and don'ts in,
    170–171
overview of, 166–167
Moving On stage
description of, 136
drivers of, 174–175
employee behaviors in, 175–176
employees in, 174
employer-sponsored support
    services in, 173
manager dos and don'ts in,
    175–176
overview of, 173–174
Multitasking, 193

N
Nonverbal communication, 191
Nonverbal language, 30–31

O
Opportunities, 32
Organizational branding, 56, 168
Organizational culture
attitudes, 25–26
beliefs, 27
definition of, 25
expectations, 28–29
importance of, 38–39
individuals and, relationship
    between, 39–42
knowledge, 29–30
language, 30–31
manager's role in, 42–46
materials, 34–35
opportunities, 32
schematic diagram of, 35
self-assessment of, 36–38
structure, 33
values, 27–28
Organizational image, 13–14,
    83–84, 168
Organizational management, 56

P
Performance management
in Decline step, 102
in Getting Settled stage, 148
in Growth step, 94
in Mission Accomplished
    stage, 168
in Moving On stage, 175
in Re-engagement or Disengage-
    ment turning point, 124
in Riding the Tide stage, 161
in Stable step, 74

Persistence, 195–196
Personal beliefs, 28
Personal issues, 194–195
Priority setting, 212, 216
Processes and procedures, 33
Professional employees, 20
Progress notes, 215

R
"Reality check," 53
Re-engagement or Disengagement
    turning point
  decision making, 121
  description of, 53
  drivers of, 123–124
  employee behaviors in, 126–127
  employees in, 123
  manager dos and don'ts, 127–129
  overview of, 121–123
Respect, 193–194
Riding the Tide stage
  description of, 136
  drivers of, 161–161
  employee behaviors in, 161–163
  employees in, 160
  manager dos and don'ts in,
    163–164
  overview of, 159
  stability as focus of, 161
Role model
  ability or willingness to change by,
    194–195
  awareness by, of what people
    value, 197–198
  characteristics of, 190–200
  communication by, 191
  employee behaviors modeled
    by, 191
  fear avoidance by, 198–199

  focus by, 195
  as knowledgeable, 192–193
  learning and development
    promotion by, 199–200
  listening by, 190–191
  manager as, 186–190
  persistence by, 195–196
  respect by, 193–194
  responsibilities of, 186
  self-assessments, 187–189
  support from, 194–195
  valuing diversity by, 192

S
Self-assessments
  manager behavior. *See* Manager
    behavior self-assessments
  manager engagement, 201–203
Sense of purpose, 10
SMART model, 212
Stable step
  description of, 53
  drivers of, 74
  employee behaviors in, 74–76
  employees in, 73
  manager dos and don'ts in, 76–77
  overview of, 73
Starting Out step
  description of, 51–53
  drivers, 56–57
  employee behaviors during, 57–58
  employees in, 56
  manager dos and don'ts in, 59–64
  overview of, 55–56
Statistics, 19–22
Stay or Leave turning point
  description of, 53
  drivers of, 112–113
  employee behaviors in, 113–115

employees in, 112
manager dos and don'ts in,
116–117
overview of, 111–112
Steady One, 43–45
Strategy, 209
Structure, 33

T

Testing the Waters step
description of, 53
drivers used in, 65–66
employee behaviors in, 66–68
employees in, 65
manager dos and don'ts in, 68–71
overview of, 64–65
Thinking ahead, 208–209
Total rewards
in Critical Incidents turning
point, 85
description of, 13
in Just Beginning stage, 140
in Re-engagement or Disengagement turning point, 123
in Riding the Tide stage, 160
in Starting Out step, 56
in Stay or Leave turning point,
112–113
in Testing the Waters step, 65
Transformer, 44–45
Trends, 19–22
Trust, 189

U

Unwritten rules, 30

V

Values
organizational culture and, 27–28
of people, role model awareness
of, 197–198
Values statement, 27–28
Valuing diversity, 192

W

"Wait-and-see" attitude, 124
Well-being, of employees, 23
Workforce diversity, 192
Workplace
emotional connection to, 167
environment of, 74

HOW TO PURCHASE ASTD PRESS PRODUCTS

All ASTD Press titles may be purchased through ASTD's online store at **www.store.astd.org**.

ASTD Press products are available worldwide through various outlets and booksellers. In the United States and Canada, individuals may also purchase titles (print or eBook) from:

Amazon– www.amazon.com (USA); www.amazon.com (CA)
Google Play– play.google.com/store
EBSCO– www.ebscohost.com/ebooks/home

Outside the United States, English-language ASTD Press titles may be purchased through distributors (divided geographically).

United Kingdom, Continental Europe, the Middle East, North Africa, Central Asia, and Latin America:
Eurospan Group
Phone: 44.1767.604.972
Fax: 44.1767.601.640
Email: eurospan@turpin-distribution.com
Web: www.eurospanbookstore.com
For a complete list of countries serviced via Eurospan please visit www.store.astd.org or email publications@astd.org.

South Africa:
Knowledge Resources
Phone: +27(11)880-8540
Fax: +27(11)880-8700/9829
Email: mail@knowres.co.za
Web: http://www.kr.co.za
For a complete list of countries serviced via Knowledge Resources please visit www.store.astd.org or email publications@astd.org.

Nigeria:
Paradise Bookshops
Phone: 08033075133
Email: paradisebookshops@gmail.com
Website: www.paradisebookshops.com

Asia:
Cengage Learning Asia Pte. Ltd.
Email: asia.info@cengage.com
Web: www.cengageasia.com
For a complete list of countries serviced via Cengage Learning please visit www.store.astd.org or email publications@astd.org.

India:
Cengage India Pvt. Ltd.
Phone: 011 43644 1111
Fax: 011 4364 1100
Email: asia.infoindia@cengage.com

For all other countries, customers may send their publication orders directly to ASTD. Please visit: **www.store.astd.org**.